Series / Number 07-081

CONTEXTUAL ANALYSIS

GUDMUND R. IVERSEN
Swarthmore College

SAGE PUBLICATIONS
The International Professional Publishers
Newbury Park   London   New Delhi

For information address:

SAGE Publications, Inc.
2455 Teller Road
Newbury Park, California 91320

SAGE Publications Ltd.
6 Bonhill Street
London EC2A 4PU
United Kingdom

SAGE Publications India Pvt. Ltd.
M-32 Market
Greater Kailash I
New Delhi 110 048 India

Printed in the United States of America

Iversen, Gudmund R.
    Contextual analysis/ Gudmund R. Iversen.
        p.   cm.—(Quantitative applications in the social sciences; 81)
    Includes bibliographical references (p.   ).
    ISBN 0-8039-4272-9 (p)
    1. Social groups—Research—Methodology.   2. Small groups—
Research—Methodology.   3. Social groups—Research—Statistical
methods.   4. Small groups—Research—Statistical methods.
I. Title.   II. Series: Sage university papers series.   Quantitative
applications in the social sciences; 81.
HM131.I89   1991
302.3—dc20   91-22014

FIRST PRINTING, 1991

Sage Production Editor: Diane S. Foster

When citing a university paper, please use the proper form. Remember to cite the current Sage University Paper series title and include the paper number. One of the following formats can be adapted (depending on the style manual used):

(1) IVERSEN, G. R. (1991) Contextual analysis. Sage University Paper Series on Quantitative Applications in the Social Sciences, 07-081. Newbury Park, CA: Sage.

OR

(2) Iversen, G. R. (1991). *Contextual Analysis* (Sage University Paper Series on Quantitative Applications in the Social Sciences, series no. 07-081). Newbury Park, CA: Sage.

CONTENTS

SERIES EDITOR'S INTRODUCTION

We may analyze data at one level—individual, group, organization, community, nation—or across levels. The second is riskier. Aggregate-data analysts must guard against the ecological fallacy, and avoid unwarranted inferences to individual behavior. After all, groups are not individuals. However, groups influence individuals. Neighborhoods, classrooms, friends, churches, constituencies, and families, to name a few, may define a group context that profoundly shapes individual behavior. Professor Iversen discusses these and other examples in his lucid explication of *contextual analysis,* the systematic study of group effects on individuals.

The technique is widely relevant, touching on research questions in all the social sciences. Professor Iversen first develops the *absolute-effects model.* Consider an illustration. Psychologist Mary Amber hypothesizes that individual final-exam performance in her "Intro 101" course is a linear function of the student's general ability, plus the intellectual quality of the assigned discussion group,

$$P = b_0 + b_1 A + b_2 G$$

where P = individual final exam score, A = the student's own G.P.A., and G = the average G.P.A. for the students in the discussion group.

The regression estimates from this equation—b_1 and b_2—suggest, respectively, the individual and group effects on exam performance. Why this interpretation? In step-by-step fashion, aided by splendid graphics, Professor Iversen explains. Then, he discusses the limitations of such an absolute-effects model. A particular problem is the high collinearity that plagues these models, making it difficult to disentangle effects, to assert that the group effect is more important than the individual effect or vice versa.

An alternative is the less common *relative-effects model,* which virtually eliminates any collinearity, making the independent variables little, if at all, correlated. Thus, effects, measured in terms of contributions to sums of squares, can be disentangled. However, this approach rests on a "centering" strategy that carries its own concerns. More generally, a relative model can lead to an interpretation of effects different from an absolute model, and it is not always clear which model should be chosen. Nevertheless, the relative approach is an insightful attempt to model context and solve the collinearity problem at the same time. This is but one instance of the creativity Professor Iversen brings to his subject.

—Michael S. Lewis-Beck
Series Editor

CONTEXTUAL ANALYSIS

GUDMUND R. IVERSEN
Swarthmore College

1. INTRODUCTION

The role of the group has long been an important part of social theory and research. Indeed, one of the classic books in the American sociological literature is aptly entitled *The Human Group* (Homans, 1950). One aspect of group research is the study of the functioning and dynamics of the group itself. Another aspect is the study of the impact of the group on the individuals that belong to the group. In this latter type of research, the focus is on the group as a *context* for the individuals in the group.

The context of a group is believed to affect the actions and attitudes of the individuals who belong to the group. Contextual analysis is the study of the role of the group context on actions and attitudes of individuals. We find an early example of such contextual analysis going back as far as Durkheim's study of suicide.

Here we are concerned with some of the statistical issues that arise in contextual analysis. Contextual analysis is possible when we have data on individuals as well as data on the groups to which they belong. Typically, we have a dependent variable measured on the individuals, and we want to study the effects of characteristics of the individuals themselves as well as characteristics of the groups to which they belong. Most of the time we want to find out what the form is of the effect of the individual and the group variables. We want to find out whether the effects are positive or negative, and we want to find out whether the effects are linear or nonlinear. We also are interested in whether the individual and group characteristics act together to produce interaction effects. In addition to the form of the relationships, we want to study how large the effects are as well as which variables (individual or group) are more important.

AUTHOR'S NOTE: *I am indebted to Lawrence H. Boyd, Jr. and Hartmut Esser for all they have taught me about this topic, and to two referees for making the book much better.*

3

As a long-term goal, we seek to go beyond the statistical analysis and obtain a better understanding of the process by which individuals are affected by the group context.

One task in a contextual analysis consists of identifying the group or groups that are thought to be relevant. As individuals we are members of many different types of groups; we belong to a family, a neighborhood, a county, a state, and a nation. Cutting across this classification, we are members of a class in school, a work group, an occupation, voluntary organizations, a parish church, a friendship group, and so forth. We are also all part of one of two very large groups: females and males.

Another task consists of identifying the relevant variables. In a contextual analysis this means identifying and measuring variables on the individuals as well as the groups used in the study. The group variables can be variables aggregated from the individual variables. For example, the group mean of a variable measured on the individuals can be used as a group variable. It also is possible to use group means of variables that are not used on the individual level as variables on the group level. Group variables also can be categorical (i.e., type of government when the groups consist of countries), and in that case they are included in the analysis as dummy variables.

Issues in Contextual Analyses

Group Boundaries. Because groups play such a large role in the lives of individuals, there are many conceptual problems that arise any time we study human groups. One problem is that some groups are well defined with fixed boundaries (i.e., a class in a school where the group consists of a certain number of students in a classroom). Other groups have fuzzy boundaries (i.e., a friendship group contains members who range from very close friends to casual acquaintances). Although in groups with fuzzy boundaries we have a continuum of degree of membership in the groups, the analysis requires us to create a dichotomy, such that some people are members of the group and the rest of the people are not members of the group. The problem consists of choosing the cutoff point on such a continuum. Even after the cutoff point is defined, there are reasons to believe that people with lower values on the continuum are less affected by the group than people with higher values. So far we have no satisfactory way of building this phenomenon into a statistical model.

Mobility. Another problem we face when we create groups to be used in a contextual analysis is that people constantly move in and out of groups. In a mobile society one student may have just entered a particular class in school, whereas others have been in the class the entire year. The same problem of new members holds for groups like neighborhoods, voluntary organizations, church groups, and so on. New members will not have been in the group long enough to have been affected by the group context to the same extent that old members have been affected. One possible solution to this problem is to include length of time spent in the group as an individual-level explanatory variable in the analysis. People also move out of groups, and we usually miss obtaining data on those individuals who have moved out and who potentially have been most affected by the group because they had been members of the group for a longer time.

Overlapping Groups. A third and potentially more serious conceptual problem is that groups overlap. For example, it may be tempting to use census tracts as the groups in a contextual analysis because of the easy availability of group data for such units. That way we tap into geographic proximity as a group phenomenon. At the same time, because of occupational, racial, religious, and other types of segregation, people tend to cluster near people similar to themselves. Therefore, it may well be that the types of groups that are important for our study are not the census tracts. Perhaps church membership really is the variable we should have used. But members of a particular congregation live scattered across many census tracts. In each tract they are mixed in with members of other congregations, even though there may be higher concentrations of members of a particular congregation in some tracts than in others. Superimposed on the census tracts and the congregations are groups defined by other variables, like type of education and income, that may be relevant for the analysis.

Sorting out and defining the relevant groups becomes difficult because people belong to so many overlapping groups. In a contextual analysis it is very hard to know if we have tapped into the right group definitions or not. This problem of group definitions may in the end become a factor that will limit the use of contextual analyses, in spite of their appeal from a substantive and statistical point of view.

Data Needs. A more practical problem with contextual analysis is that it is a very data-intensive proposition to get into. The statistical models require that we have data on individuals as well as on the groups to which they belong. The individual data are often obtained from sample surveys. Some characteristics of the groups can be obtained by aggregating the individual data across the groups. In addition, the analysis is usually more informative when we have other types of data on the groups. This means that the collection of the group data has to be part of the original design of the study and not something that is thought of and done separately at a later stage. It also means that the collection of the individual-level data has to be done within the groups we plan to use and not simply across a city or a state or the nation the way most surveys of individuals are done. For one thing, we have to make certain that the number of observations within each group is large enough to permit a meaningful statistical analysis within each group. Thus, a contextual analysis places greater demand on the study design than most other types of social research. A direct consequence of this is that the cost of the data collection tends to be high.

Missing Individual Data. A related data problem in contextual analysis is that of missing individual data. There are times when the group data are readily available, but it is hard to collect the corresponding individual data. In an election, for example, we have data from a district of how many people voted for each of the parties. At the same time, we may have census data on the religious composition of the district. These group data come from aggregating data on the individuals in the groups. Correlating these group variables across a set of districts gives us the aggregate correlation. There is no reason to believe that we would have obtained the same value of the correlation coefficient if we could correlate the same variables using individual-level data, and we cannot commit the ecological fallacy of interpreting the group correlation as applying to the individuals. But this raises the question of whether it is possible, in some way or other, to recover the individual-level data that produced the aggregate data in the first place.

The basic answer to that question is that it is not possible to recover the individual-level data. In its most simple case, imagine we have a contingency table with two rows and two columns, and we know the row and column totals, but the four cell entries are missing. The row and column totals are the group data, and the missing cell entries make up the individual-level data. There are now many different ways we can fill in the four cell entries and still have the same totals in such a table because of the one degree of freedom associated with the four cell entries, and we do not know which of the many possible sets of cell entries is the correct one.

A modified answer to the question of whether we can recover missing individual-level data is that such recovery is possible if we are willing to make certain assumptions about the structure of the missing data. Because the data are missing, we have no way of assessing from the data themselves whether these assumptions are correct. Thus, these assumptions must come from other knowledge we have about the data. Sometimes it may be possible to recover missing individual-level data if we already have partial individual-level data. For example, it may be that we have aggregate data for all the groups, as well as individual, survey data for some of the groups. For a further discussion of this topic and the types of assumptions that are needed, see Boyd and Iversen (1979) and Iversen (1981).

Choice of Models. Any statistical analysis of data depends on both the data and the model that is used for the analysis of the data. This also is true for contextual analysis, even though the current choice of models is small. The most commonly used statistical model is a contextual analysis with absolute effects (see Chapter 3). A contextual model with relative effects is discussed in Chapter 4. Both of these models make use of regression analysis. In addition, we have to make a choice between considering the regression coefficients as fixed parameters or as random variables. The models in Chapters 3 and 4 are based on fixed parameters; random parameters are discussed in Chapter 7. The impact of the difficulties with contextual analysis discussed above may be so large that the choice between fixed and random regression coefficients may not be all that important.

The Literature

Statistical Theory. The formal statistical analysis of contextual effects started with the analysis of contingency tables. Early examples of this type of analysis are found in Kendall and Lazarsfeld (1950) and in P. M. Blau (1960). More recent discussions of models for contextual analysis are found, among others, in Alpheis (1988), where he reports on an empirical study and gives a review of theoretical issues in contextual analysis, in Blalock's (1984) article on theoretical and methodological issues in contextual analysis, and in Boyd and Iversen's (1979) book on contextual analysis.

Other discussions of statistical issues are in Eulau's (1981) article, where he discusses how to link the behavior of individuals with the larger groups to which they belong, Goldstein's (1987) book on multilevel analysis, in O'Brien and Roach's (1984) article stressing the importance of contextual analyses in urban sociology, in Stipak and Hensler's (1982) article for political scientists on statistical issues in contextual analysis, and in van den Eeden and Hüttner's (1982) overview of multilevel research in an entire issue of *Current Sociology*. Hauser (1970) warns against committing the contextual fallacy of concluding that contextual effects are present when people are located in groups by some process related to the dependent variable, artificially producing group effects.

Substantive Applications. In view of the discussion about the problems of defining the groups that are to be used in a contextual analysis, it is not surprising to find that educational research may well be the major user of contextual-analysis methods. The advantage of studying students in a school setting is, of course, that the students come in classes that serve as well-defined groups. A difficulty arises when the students meet as one group in their homeroom and then form other groups as they study different subjects. One way around that is to treat the entire grade in a school as a group. Educational data are well structured on several levels; classes are part of grades that are part of schools that are part of school districts, and so on. Also, a good deal of educational data is gathered as test scores as part of the regular evaluation of the students, which means that the problems of data collection are not as severe as for many other types of studies.

Examples of educational contextual analyses of students are found in Engel (1988), who studies status inconsistency with the classroom as the group context. Raudenbush and Bryk (1986) do separate analyses within each school and examine the resulting regression coefficients in their hierarchical model for the study of school effects. In their statistical model they present a modified Bayesian estimation method. Other examples of educational research are found in Treiber (1980, 1981), studying German schools, in Waxman and Eash (1983), in Wienold et al. (1982), in Wiese (1986), studying German schools, in Willms and Cuttance (1985), studying Scottish schools, and in Willms (1986), studying Scottish schools. Another paper in an educational setting by Holzemer et al. (1989) contains a summary of a study of nursing faculty, with an overview of contextual analysis and a summary of a study of the mental health of head nurses. A review of educational contextual analysis shows a strong international flavor with many activities in countries like Germany, Great Britain, and the Netherlands.

Neighborhoods are another type of group often used in contextual research. Apple and O'Brien (1983) use neighborhoods in their study of the extent to which attitudes toward the evaluation of police performance are affected by the racial composition of the neighborhood. They found different effects for blacks and whites. Esser (1982, 1986) uses neighborhoods in his studies of foreign workers in Germany, and Fernandez and Kulik (1981) use neighborhoods in their multilevel study of life satisfaction. Gates and Rohe (1987) use six Atlanta neighborhoods in a study of reactions to crime as influenced by neighborhood physical characteristics and crime rates, individual characteristics, neighborhood social context, perceived neighborhood conditions, perceived informal social control, and crime-related perceptions.

Other examples of the use of neighborhoods include the study by Mueller and O'Brien (1986) on the relationship between utilization of public services and neighborhood racial composition, and the study by Simcha-Fagan and Schwartz (1986) on self-reported and officially reported delinquency as they relate to contextual effects of the neighborhoods, level of organizational participation, and the extent of disorder and criminal subcultures. Smith and Jarjoura (1989) have data on more than 9,000 households in 57 neighborhoods for household burglaries as a function of attributes of individual households and neighborhood characteristics, and Stipak (1980) uses survey and census data from the Detroit metropolitan area to analyze the effect of the neighborhood racial composition on the residents' satisfaction with their neighborhoods. Entwisle, Casterline, and Sayed (1989) use Egyptian villages as their groups in a study of the villages as contexts for the use of contraceptives. Going beyond a strict definition of neighborhood R. R. Blau (1988) uses the primary sampling unit as the contextual group in a study of attendance at cultural activities.

Another type of group for which data are readily available is the census tract; Hero and Durand (1985) use such tracts in their study of how people evaluate urban services, and Usui and Keil (1987) use census tracts to study life satisfaction. Cities are used by Schissel, Wanner, and Frieders (1989) in their study of attitudes toward immigrants in Canada. Aspin (1988) uses groups of pairs of countries as the group in an unconventional contextual analysis of power and foreign policy behavior.

Political scientists naturally turn to election districts as possible groups in their contextual analyses. C. Brown (1982) uses German election results in a national ecological study of the Nazi vote, and T. Brown (1981) uses election districts and counties in a study of attributes and contextual change. Lancaster and Lewis-Beck (1989) use geographic areas in Spain as their groups in a study of regional vote support, and Mastekaasa and Moum (1984) use counties to study the perceived quality of life in Norway. County data also are used by Prysby (1989) in the study of attitudes toward Jesse Jackson.

Other studies make use of a variety of types of groups. The family as a group is used by Hauser and Mossel (1985) in a study of occupational status as a function of schooling. The data are analyzed using a structural model in the LISREL framework. Voluntary organizations are used by Knoke (1981) in a study of commitment and detachment. Leege and Welch (1989) use the parish to which an individual belongs in their study of Catholics and their parish context. Wald, Owen, and Hill (1988) also use churches as groups in their study of political conservatism as a function of individual and group characteristics. Markham (1988) uses metal processing firms as groups in a study of whether performance affects pay in order to demonstrate the presence of group effects. Huckfeldt and Sprague (1987) use social networks as groups in their study of the flow of political information. Their study was carefully designed to allow for the analysis of group effects.

These examples of contextual analyses illustrate the wide range of groups that are used in the literature. The examples do not show quite as well the wide range of substantive issues that are considered in these articles. As we would expect, the articles come from journals in education, sociology, and political science. But they also come from journals in police science, urban affairs, nursing, religious research, psychology, migration, criminology, and so forth. This range of areas illustrates how broadly contextual analysis has been used in the study of human behavior.

2. CONTINGENCY TABLES

Contextual analysis of a set of contingency tables serves to introduce several of the issues we face when we do a contextual analysis, even though contingency tables are no longer commonly used in contextual analyses. We seldom have categorical variables only, and when we have a mix of variables we replace the categorical variables by dummy variables and use regression analysis.

The simplest case of contextual analysis occurs when we have data on two categorical variables X and Y, and each variable has only two categories. When we have data on these two variables for several groups of individuals, then we can do a contextual analysis on the data on these two variables.

For a particular group the data can be arranged in a two-by-two contingency table, as shown in Table 2.1. The two variables X and Y are also shown as dummy variables with values 0 and 1.

TABLE 2.1
Data on Two Variables Arranged in a Contingency Table

		X		
		0	1	Sum
	1	n_{11}	n_{12}	$n_{1.}$
Y	0	n_{21}	n_{22}	$n_{2.}$
	Sum	$n_{.1}$	$n_{.2}$	n

The frequencies in Table 2.1 can be used to compute the proportions shown in Table 2.2. We get the column proportions by dividing the frequencies in a given column by the total for that column. In addition to the proportions in Table 2.2, we also need the two marginal column proportions $p_{.1} = n_{.1}/n$ and $p_{.2} = n_{.2}/n$ for the analysis.

There is a relationship between the two variables in a particular group if the two column proportions p_{11} and p_{12} are different from

TABLE 2.2
Proportions Computed from the Frequencies in Table 2.1

		X		
		0	1	Sum
	1	p_{11}	p_{12}	$p_1.$
Y	0	p_{21}	p_{22}	$p_2.$
	Sum	1.00	1.00	1.00

each other. When the two variables are related, an individual's value of X partly determines an individual's value of Y. This is expressed by saying that there is an effect of X on Y on the individual level. Alternatively, we can say there is an individual-level effect of X on Y.

An individual's value of Y also can be affected by the context of the group to which the individual belongs. To study such a contextual effect we need data on at least two groups, meaning that we need two contingency tables. Data on two groups are shown in the two contingency tables in Table 2.3.

TABLE 2.3
Data on X and Y for Two Groups

		X						
		Group 1				Group 2		
		0	1	Sum		0	1	Sum
Y	1	0.70	0.70	0.70	1	0.40	0.40	0.40
	0	0.30	0.30	0.30	0	0.60	0.60	0.60
	Sum	1.00	1.00	1.00	Sum	1.00	1.00	1.00

First, let us suppose there is no individual-level effect of X on Y in either of the two groups. This means the two column proportions are equal to each other in each of the tables. Because two column proportions p_{11} and p_{12} are equal in a particular table, it makes no difference for the value of Y whether an individual has the value 0 or 1 on X. In the example in Table 2.3, we see that in the first table 70% of the individuals have Y equal to 1 for both X equal to 0 and to 1. Similarly, in the second group 40% have Y equal to 1 for both X equal to 0 and to 1. Thus, knowing an individual's value of X does not help us predict what the value is of Y. This means there is no individual-level effect of X on Y in either of the groups.

However, there is a group effect present in these data. If we are told that an individual belongs to the first group, then we know that 70% of those people have Y equal to 1. Similarly, if we are told that an individual belongs to the second group, we know that only 40% have Y equal to 1. Because the two percentages are different, there is a group effect on Y in these data. This also can be seen in terms of prediction. If we are told that an individual belongs to Group 1, then we would predict that $Y = 1$ for this individual. Using this prediction we would be correct 70% of the time. Similarly, if we are told that an individual belongs to Group 2, then we would predict that $Y = 0$, and we would be correct 60% of the time.

Contextual analysis is based on the notion that we have data on two or more variables for several groups, and we want to study these data for the presence of individual and group effects. In this case it means we have several contingency tables showing the relationship between X and Y.

Following Davis, Spaeth, and Huson (1961), the first thing we do is to plot the two column proportions p_{11} and p_{12} as functions of the marginal proportion $p_{.2}$. The marginal proportion is a characteristic of the group, and it tells us the proportion of individuals in each group that has X equal to 1. The two column proportions in each group tell us the proportions of individuals that have Y equal to 1 for each value of X. The purpose of the graph is to see if the composition of the group in any way relates to proportions of individuals that have Y equal to 1.

Figure 2.1 (not based on data from Table 2.3) shows a linear relationship between the two column proportions and the marginal proportion. The graph shows that as the marginal proportion of people with $X = 1$ goes up in the groups, there are more people with $Y = 1$ for both values of X. The graph also shows that the column proportion p_{11} is higher than the column proportion p_{12}. This means that the proportion of people with $Y = 1$ is higher for people with $X = 0$ than for people with $X = 1$.

To make this more concrete, suppose each table represents an election precinct. The variable X is the party registration of a person and Y is the party vote. Let 0 represent Republican and 1 represent Democrat. The graph then says that as the proportion of registered Democrats goes up, the more both Republicans and Democrats vote Democratic. This is seen from the positive slopes of the two lines in

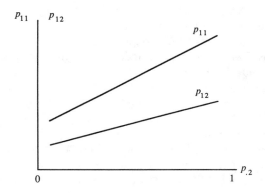

Figure 2.1. Linear Relationships Between the Column Proportions and the Marginal Proportion

the graph. The fact that the two lines are not parallel and that the top line is steeper than the bottom line tells us that as the proportion of registered Democrats in the precinct goes up, the Republicans increase their Democratic vote faster than the registered Democrats do. Finally, the fact that one line lies above the other tells us that in any precinct the proportion of Republicans voting the Democratic ticket is larger than the proportion of Democrats voting the Democratic ticket. As we know, anything is possible in American politics.

Statistical Model

When this plot of column proportions against the marginal proportion shows linear trends, then we can represent the lines by equations, as shown by Iversen (1973). Here the two lines in Figure 2.1 are represented by the following two equations:

$$p_{11} = \alpha + \beta p_{.2} \qquad [2.1]$$

$$p_{12} = \gamma + \delta p_{.2} \qquad [2.2]$$

The intercepts and slopes of the lines are shown using Greek letters. The intercepts and slopes are known as the parameters for the two lines. When we have actual data on several groups and make scatter plots of the column proportions against the marginal proportion, then we would not get points that lie exactly on two straight lines. In that case, we introduce residual terms in the two equations. This situation is discussed further below.

The four parameters tell us about the presence of the individual and group effects in the data. To see this, let us discuss several different possibilities. In particular, let us see what happens if one or more of the parameters are equal to 0.

If the two slopes β and δ are both equal to 0, then the two lines will be horizontal. In that case it does not matter for the column proportions p_{11} and p_{12} what group a person belongs to, because p_{11} is the same in every group and p_{12} is the same in every group. Thus, the group composition, as measured by $p_{.2}$, has no effect on the column proportions. If the two lines are horizontal and the two intercepts α and γ are different, then the two column proportions differ from each other in each group. In that case it matters for Y whether a person is in the first or second column. But it does not matter what group the person is in. Thus, two horizontal lines are a sign that there is only an individual level effect of X on Y, and there is no group effect.

Another possibility is that the two lines have a nonzero slope and that they overlap. In that case the two column proportions are equal to each other in each group, but this common value changes as we move across the groups. This means that it only matters for Y what group a person is in. In this case it does not matter what column the person is in.

Because the two ps are equal in any given table, it means there is no individual effect present. But with a nonzero slope for the two lines, the common value of the ps differs from one table to the next, and this means it matters for Y what group a person belongs to. Thus, there is a group effect present in this case.

It is now possible to have lines that show both individual and group level effects. The individual effect creates lines with different intercepts, and the group effect creates parallel lines with nonzero slopes.

Finally, the last possibility is that both intercepts and slopes are different. When this is the case, there is an individual-group interaction effect present in addition to the possible individual and group effects.

This discussion can be translated into statements about the four parameters. Only the individual effect of X on Y is present when the lines are horizontal ($\beta = \delta = 0$) and the intercepts differ ($\alpha \neq \gamma$). Only the group effect is present when the intercepts are equal ($\alpha = \gamma$) and the slopes are equal ($\beta = \delta \neq 0$). In that case the two lines coincide and have nonzero slopes.

So far we have discussed the parameters in terms of the relationships between the marginal proportion and the two column proportions. It also is possible to discuss the four parameters in a regression setting studying the relationship between the two variables Y and X. Having established the way in which Y is related to X for contingency tables, it also is possible to generalize the analysis to the case where both Y and X are metric instead of categorical variables.

Within Group Regressions

To express the relationship between Y and X in an equation for a particular group, we make use of the fact that in the tables above the two variables X and Y also are represented by dummy variables with the values 0 and 1. If we use these dummy variables and regress Y on X within a group, we get the following equation for the regression line for that group:

$$Y = p_{11} + (p_{12} - p_{11}) X \qquad [2.3]$$

The intercept for the regression line becomes the column proportion p_{11} and the slope becomes the difference between the two column proportions, $p_{12} - p_{11}$.

It is now possible to discuss the slope and intercept of this line in terms of the four parameters α, β, γ, and δ. According to Equation 2.1, we have the intercept p_{11} in Equation 2.3 expressed as a linear function of the marginal proportion, as seen in the equation

$$p_{11} = \alpha + \beta\, p_{.2} . \qquad [2.4]$$

If we subtract Equation 2.2 from Equation 2.1 we get the slope, meaning the difference $p_{12} - p_{11}$ between the two column proportions expressed in the equation

$$p_{12} - p_{11} = (\gamma - \alpha) + (\delta - \beta)\, p_{.2} . \qquad [2.5]$$

Using the dummy variable for X we find that the mean of X equals the marginal proportion $p_{.2}$. Now we have both the intercept and the slope in Equation 2.3 expressed in terms of the mean of X and the four parameters.

So far, Equation 2.3 relates Y to X within a particular group. With J groups we have J different regression analyses. However, it also is possible to relate Y to X in one single analysis using data in all the groups. To see this we can substitute Equations 2.4 and 2.5 in Equation 2.3. This gives us the equation

$$Y = \alpha + (\gamma - \alpha) X + \beta \, p_{.2} + (\delta - \beta) X p_{.2} , \qquad [2.6]$$

which relates the dependent dummy variable Y across all the groups to the X variable and the marginal proportions $p_{.2}$.

In the case when there is only an individual level effect present, we know from the discussion above that the lines in Figure 2.1 are horizontal ($\beta = \delta = 0$) and the intercepts differ ($\alpha \neq \gamma$). In this case the intercept (p_{11}) is equal to the constant α. Similarly, the slope ($p_{12} - p_{11}$) is equal to the constant $\gamma - \alpha$. This means the column proportions are the same in all the tables, but p_{12} and p_{11} are different from each other. By definition, this is the case of the individual effect of X on Y.

In the case of only a group effect being present, we know from the discussion above that for the lines in Figure 2.1 the intercepts are equal ($\alpha = \gamma$) and the slopes are equal ($\beta = \delta \neq 0$). In this case the intercept (p_{11}) is a linear function of the marginal proportion $p_{.2}$. Similarly, the slope within each group ($p_{12} - p_{11}$) equals 0. Because this effect is produced by the marginal proportion $p_{.2}$, which is the mean of X, we say that this group effect is the group effect of the variable X. Group effects also can be due to variables other than X, but here we only discuss the case when the group effect is due to X.

Both individual and group effects are present when $\alpha \neq \gamma$ and $\beta = \delta \neq 0$. In that case the intercepts vary from one group to the next. But the slopes are the same, meaning that the regression lines within the groups are parallel. When the lines are not parallel, there is an individual-group interaction effect present as well.

We learn two things from this section. First, when we use dummy variables for the two variables that define a two-by-two contingency table, we can analyze the relationship between the two variables by regressing one variable on the other within each group. Second, if the column proportions are linearly related to the marginal proportion of X, then we can express the intercept and slope of the regression lines for the two-by-two table as linear functions of the marginal proportion

TABLE 3.1
Data Matrix with Dependent and Independent Variables, Together
with Group Membership

Y	X	Group
y_{11}	x_{11}	1
y_{21}	x_{21}	1
.	.	.
.	.	.
.	.	.
y_{ij}	x_{ij}	j
.	.	.
.	.	.
.	.	.

of X. Because this proportion is the mean of X, we find that the intercepts and slopes within the groups can be expressed as linear functions of the mean of X. In the next chapter we use these results to study the presence of individual, group, and interaction effects when the two variables X and Y are metric (interval) variables.

3. CONTEXTUAL ANALYSIS WITH ABSOLUTE EFFECTS

In contextual analysis we want to study the effect of an independent variable X and the group context on a dependent variable Y. This means we need data on several individuals as well as data on the groups to which these individuals belong. In the most simple case the data matrix looks like the matrix shown in Table 3.1. The table shows values on X and Y as well as what groups the individuals belong to. Group membership is the only group variable introduced so far. In the data matrix the second subscript on X and Y refers to the group number, and the first subscript refers to the individual within the group. The contextual model discussed in this section forms the basis for the work by Boyd and Iversen (1979).

To study the relationship between X and Y we can first make a scatterplot of X and Y for all the data. If this relationship looks linear, it can be analyzed using simple regression analysis. But it may be that

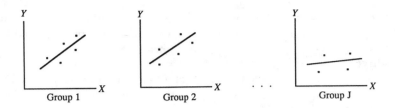

Figure 3.1. Scatterplots and Regression Lines for *J* Groups

the relationship between X and Y is not the same in each group. In that case the overall scatterplot does not give a very good representation of how X and Y are related, and we ought to take the group variable into account in the analysis.

To examine the possibility that X and Y are not related the same way in each group we control for the group variable. This is done by dividing the data into groups, such that we can make a separate scatterplot of Y on X for each group. Suppose we get different scatterplots and relationships for the various groups, as shown in Figure 3.1.

The scatterplots show us that Y is not related to X in the same way for every group. The groups have different intercepts as well as different slopes. In this case a single scatterplot for all the data does not give a good representation of the way in which X and Y are related. An overall scatterplot would show a very low correlation between the two variables. However, when we make separate scatterplots for the groups, there is a strong relationship between the two variables within each group. Here it seems as if there is something about the groups themselves that influences the way in which the two variables are related. Thus, we should take the group explicitly into account in the analysis.

The group variable is explicitly taken into account by first analyzing the relationship between Y and X within each group. When these relationships are linear, we can do a separate linear regression analysis for each group. The regression model for this analysis in the *j*th group can be expressed in the equation

$$y_{ij} = \delta_{0j} + \delta_{1j} x_{ij} + \varepsilon_{ij} \qquad j = 1, 2, \ldots, J. \qquad [3.1]$$

The intercepts within the groups are called δ_0 and the slopes are called δ_1. We now have a set of J different intercepts $\delta_{01}, \delta_{02}, \ldots,$

δ_{0J}, and we have a set of J different slopes $\delta_{11}, \delta_{12}, \ldots, \delta_{1J}$. These deltas are parameters, and we use the data in the groups to estimate these parameters. It is also possible to use more than one X variable, and everything in this chapter generalizes directly to the case of a multivariate relationship within each group.

The fact that the intercepts are different and the slopes are different from one group to the next leads directly to the question of *why* they are different. There must be some reason why the groups are different, and we want to know what it is that determines these slopes and intercepts. This question can be expressed in the model equations

$$\text{intercept } \delta_0 = \text{function of something} \qquad [3.2]$$

$$\text{slope } \delta_1 = \text{function of something} \qquad [3.3]$$

These model equations raise two issues: what kinds of functions do we have, and what variables are these functions of?

The obvious answers to these two questions are that the choices of functions and variables depend on the substantive problem at hand. Ideally, the substantive problem should dictate what variables we use to explain the differences in the intercepts and slopes, and the substantive problem also should dictate what the forms are of these equations. But, as with so much other social research, the reason we do the research is that we do not know which variables are important and we do not know the forms of the relationships. We are doing the research to find these things out.

Therefore, we start with the most simple mathematical functions, and this means linear functions. Suppose the intercepts and slopes are functions of the k variables $V_1, V_2, \ldots, V_k$, and these variables have been observed for all the groups. In that case the model equations become expressed as

$$\delta_{0j} = \alpha_0 + \alpha_2 v_{1j} + \alpha_4 v_{2j} + \ldots + \alpha_{2k} v_{kj} \qquad [3.4]$$

$$\delta_{1j} = \alpha_1 + \alpha_3 v_{1j} + \alpha_5 v_{2j} + \ldots + \alpha_{2k+1} v_{kj}. \qquad [3.5]$$

The two model equations say that the parameters in the groups are linear functions of these k group variables. As the equations are written here they do not contain any residual terms, as we typically see them in regression analysis. This means the deltas are here considered as fixed parameters. It would be possible to include residual terms in Equations 3.4 and 3.5. In that case the deltas would be considered as random parameters. For a discussion of fixed versus random regression coefficients see, for example, de Leeuw and Kreft (1986), Goldstein (1987), and Tate and Wongbundhit (1983).

The main difference between Equations 3.4 and 3.5 and ordinary regression equations is that the quantities on the left sides of the equations are parameters from some other analysis instead of observed values of a dependent variable. This is one reason for not introducing residual terms at this stage.

To use Equations 3.4 and 3.5 in a regression analysis to study the effects of the V variables, we need values for the two dependent variables, the deltas. We do this by estimating the deltas through simple regression of Y on X within each group. In the jth group the estimated intercept is denoted d_{0j} and the slope d_{1j}. With these coefficients as the dependent variables we can use Equations 3.4 and 3.5 as multiple regression equations and find the as as the estimates of the alphas. We get

$$d_{0j} = a_0 + a_2 v_{1j} + a_4 v_{2j} + \ldots + a_{2k} v_{kj} + u_j \qquad [3.6]$$

$$d_{1j} = a_1 + a_3 v_{1j} + a_5 v_{2j} + \ldots + a_{2k+1} v_{kj} + v_j. \qquad [3.7]$$

The magnitudes of the as and the R^2s in these two analyses will help us understand in what ways the Vs influence the group relationships.

Nothing has been said about the nature of the Vs. They represent characteristics of one kind or another of the groups, and there is not much limit on how many variables there can be. Some or all the variables can be categorical (nominal) variables represented by dummy variables, and in that case we get into analysis of covariance. For such an approach see Schuessler (1969). Perhaps more often the variables are group means or proportions of some kind.

Basic Model

As a special, but important case, we consider the situation where we have only one V variable influencing the group intercepts and slopes, and that variable is the group mean of the original independent variable

22

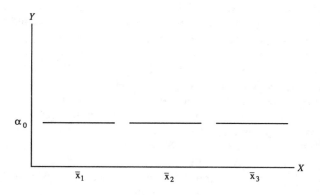

Figure 3.2. No Effects of X on Y

X. With the choice of linear functions and the group mean as the one variable, the model equations can be written

$$\delta_{0j} = \alpha_0 + \alpha_2 \bar{x}_j \qquad [3.8]$$

$$\delta_{1j} = \alpha_1 + \alpha_3 \bar{x}_j . \qquad [3.9]$$

This model states that the mean of X in group number j linearly determines the way in which Y is related to X in that group.

This is a generalization of the model used for contingency tables, where the column proportions are studied as linear functions of the marginal proportions. The contingency table model is a special case in the sense that when the independent variable in a contingency table is expressed as a 0–1 dummy variable, then the mean of that dummy variable becomes the proportion of 1s.

The alphas in Equations 3.8 and 3.9 tell us about the presence of effects of X on Y. The case of no effects of X occurs when there is no relationship between Y and X within each group, and the groups are not different from each other. This case is illustrated in Figure 3.2, which shows regression lines for Y on X for three groups. There is no effect of X on Y within each group, because the regression lines for each group are horizontal, and the slope within each group equals zero. Furthermore, there are no differences between the groups because the regression lines within the groups have the same intercept

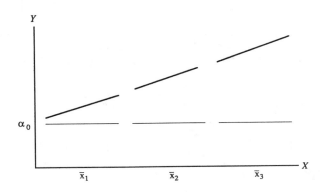

Figure 3.3. Individual-Level Effect of X on Y, with No-Effect Line for Each Group

α_0. In this case $\alpha_1 = \alpha_3 = 0$ because the slopes are all equal to zero. Also, $\alpha_2 = 0$ because all the intercepts are equal.

Let us now introduce the individual-level effect of X on Y. This means that it matters for the value of Y what the value of X is for an individual. Without the presence of a group effect it does not matter what group this individual belongs to. There are two different types of individual effects. The absolute individual effect is introduced here, and the relative individual effect is introduced in Chapter 5.

The absolute individual effect is illustrated in Figure 3.3. In this figure the regression lines have nonzero slopes. This tells us that it matters for Y what the value of X is for an individual, and we have an individual-level effect present of X on Y. The lines still have the same intercept. Figure 3.3 also includes the no-effect lines from Figure 3.2. We see that the introduction of the individual-level effect has the effect of swinging the regression lines within the groups up, as if they were connected to each other.

The parameter for the individual-level effect in this contextual analysis is therefore α_1. Note that in both Figure 3.2 and Figure 3.3 the regression lines are drawn in such a way that it looks as if there is no overlap in X values for the three groups. The only reason for drawing the graphs that way is that otherwise the lines would overlap, and we would not be able to distinguish the lines for the three groups in the graph. In most practical applications there would be an overlap in

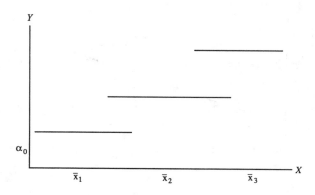

Figure 3.4. Group-Level Effect of X on Y

the values of X, and therefore the regression lines for the groups also would overlap.

There is still no group effect present of X on Y. We see this from the figure, because in order to predict Y we need only have the individual's value of X. Knowing what group an individual belongs to does not help us predict the value of Y. The reason for the name *absolute individual effect* for this model is that it is the actual value of X that determines the value of Y. As we see in Chapter 5, when there is a relative individual effect, it is the value of X relative to the mean of the group that matters for Y.

Going back to Equations 3.8 and 3.9, we see that in the case of an individual-level effect of X on Y we have $\alpha_1 \neq 0$. This means we have nonzero slopes within the groups. We also have $\alpha_2 = \alpha_3 = 0$. The meaning of $\alpha_2 = 0$ is that the intercepts for the regression lines in the groups are all equal to the common value α_0. The meaning of $\alpha_3 = 0$ is that the slopes are all equal to the common value α_1. This is exactly the situation illustrated in Figure 3.3.

Next we consider the case when there is a group-level effect present but not the individual-level effect. In that case, knowing the value of X for an individual is of no help in predicting what the corresponding value of Y is equal to, because most often the range of X values overlaps for the groups. However, if we know what group a person belongs to, we are able to predict the value of Y for that person. Figure 3.4 illustrates this

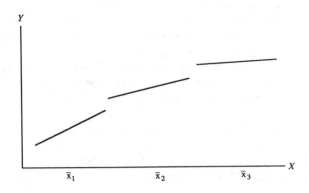

Figure 3.5. Individual, Group, and Interaction Effects

case. Within each group there is no relationship between Y and X, and the regression lines are horizontal. But the overall level of Y varies with the groups, and the regression lines for the groups have different intercepts.

From Equations 3.8 and 3.9 we see that in the case of only a group-level effect of X on Y we have $\alpha_1 = \alpha_3 = 0$. With both these two parameters equal to zero the slopes in all the regression lines are equal to zero, and the lines are all horizontal. We obtain the different intercepts when $\alpha_2 \neq 0$. The parameter for the group effect in this contextual analysis is therefore α_2.

When we have both an individual and a group effect present in our data, the regression lines for the groups are parallel and have different intercepts. It also is possible to have a case where the regression lines are not parallel. In that case, there is an individual-group interaction effect present in addition to the individual and the group effects. This case is shown in Figure 3.5. In this graph the regression lines for the groups have different intercepts, and they also have different slopes. The individual-level effect is present because Y and X are related within the groups. The group-level effect is present because the overall level of Y is different for the groups. The interaction effect is present because the lines are not parallel when we control for the group variable. Because the slopes are no longer equal, $\alpha_3 \neq 0$. Thus, the parameter for the interaction effect in this contextual analysis is α_3.

In this contextual analysis, we construct an observed value y_{ij} of the dependent variable Y as having been exposed to several different effects. The value of Y for an individual starts out being equal to α_0. Then this individual is exposed to the individual effect of X, the group effect of X, and the individual-group interaction effect of X. Finally, the individual is exposed to the residual variable. After the individual has been exposed to these four factors we find the observed value equal to y_{ij}.

We are interested in knowing how large these effects are both for a single individual and for all the individuals in the study taken together. One way to get some sense of how large these effects are is to substitute Equations 3.8 and 3.9 into Equation 3.1. This gives us the equation

$$y_{ij} = \delta_{0j} + \delta_{1j} x_{ij} + \varepsilon_{ij}$$

$$= (\alpha_0 + \alpha_2 \bar{x}_j) + (\alpha_1 + \alpha_3 \bar{x}_j) x_{ij} + \varepsilon_{ij}$$

$$= \alpha_0 + \alpha_1 x_{ij} + \alpha_2 \bar{x}_j + \alpha_3 x_{ij} \bar{x}_j + \varepsilon_{ij} \qquad [3.10]$$

$$= \text{original value} + \text{individual effect} + \text{group effect}$$
$$+ \text{interaction effect} + \text{residual effect.}$$

From Equation 3.10 we see that all the observations start with the original value of Y equal to the constant α_0. For this particular observation the individual effect of X adds the term $\alpha_1 x_{ij}$. The group effect adds the term $\alpha_2 \bar{x}_j$. The interaction effect adds the term $\alpha_3 x_{ij} \bar{x}_j$, and the residual variable adds the term ε_{ij}. Together these effects add up and produce the observed value of Y. These effects also are illustrated in Figure 3.6.

Estimation of Parameters

There are two sets of parameters in the contextual model discussed here. First, there are the deltas used to characterize the relationship between Y and X within each group. Those parameters also are used as dependent variables in the model equations. Second, there are the alphas used to model the way in which the deltas are determined. In the special case we discuss here, the alphas are

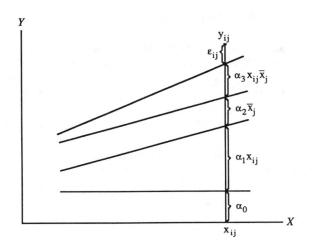

Figure 3.6. Magnitudes of Individual, Group, Interaction, and Residual Effects

the coefficients in the linear equations with the group mean as the independent variable.

The deltas can be estimated by regressing Y on X within each group. For the jth group we get the estimated relationship between Y and X expressed in the equation

$$y_{ij} = d_{0j} + d_{1j} x_{ij} + f_{ij} \qquad [3.11]$$

where the fs are the observed residuals. From these analyses we get one intercept and one slope for each group.

These estimated intercepts and slopes do not tell us anything directly about the existence of individual, group, and interaction effects. But, to the extent that the coefficients differ from group to group, we know that there are possible effects present in the data. Therefore, it is always important, as a first step, to examine the relationships between Y and X within the groups and see if they differ from group to group.

There are two main ways in which the effect parameters (alphas) can be estimated. The first method uses the group as the unit in the analysis, and is known as the *separate-equations method*. The second method uses the individual as the unit, and is known as the *single equation method.*

The separate-equations method is based on the two model equations (3.8 and 3.9). We do not have the actual deltas on the left side of those equations, but we have estimated deltas from the regression analyses within the groups and we use those estimated deltas instead of the true deltas. The difference between the true and the estimated delta becomes the residual in a regression equation that can be used to estimate the alphas.

By regressing the observed intercepts and slopes on the group means we get the following two equations,

$$d_{0j} = a_0 + a_2 \bar{x}_j + u_j \qquad [3.12]$$

$$d_{1j} = a_1 + a_3 \bar{x}_j + v_j \qquad [3.13]$$

where the us and the vs are the estimated residuals and the as are estimates of the alphas.

The unit in these two analyses is the group. Therefore, this method may not be a good way to estimate the alphas if we only have a small number of groups. When the number of individuals varies a great deal across the groups, it is better to use a weighted regression analysis and make the larger groups count more in the analysis.

The single-equation method is based on Equation 3.10. This equation shows that when we have a linear relationship between Y and X within the groups and the group intercepts and slopes are linear functions of the group means, then the value of Y for an individual is a function of the individual value of X, the group mean of X, and the product of the individual value and the group mean.

This equation can be used for estimation of the alpha parameters through a multiple regression analysis with three explanatory variables. To perform this analysis, two more columns must be constructed from the original data matrix. We already have individual values of Y and X, and we now need one column for the group variable and another for the interaction variable. The column for the group variable is constructed by assigning the group mean to every individual in that group. The column for the interaction variable is constructed by multiplying the individual and group columns. That way the data matrix looks like the table shown in Table 3.2.

TABLE 3.2

Data Matrix with Dependent, Individual, Group, and Interaction
Variables

Y	Individual	Group	Interaction
y_{11}	x_{11}	$\bar{x}_1$	$x_{11}\bar{x}_1$
y_{21}	x_{21}	$\bar{x}_1$	$x_{21}\bar{x}_1$
.	.	.	.
.	.	.	.
.	.	.	.
y_{ij}	x_{ij}	$\bar{x}_j$	$x_{ij}\bar{x}_j$
.	.	.	.
.	.	.	.
.	.	.	.

Regressing Y on the individual, group, and interaction variables results in the estimated regression equation

$$y_{ij} = A_0 + A_1 x_{ij} + A_2 \bar{x}_j + A_3 x_{ij}\bar{x}_j + e_{ij} \qquad [3.14]$$

where the As are the estimated coefficients and the es are the estimated residuals. The estimated coefficients from this single-equation analysis are denoted by capital As to distinguish these estimates from the as obtained from the separate-equations estimation.

There is commonly a good deal of collinearity present in the single-equation estimation. The individual X values are correlated with the group means, and the individual and group variables are correlated with the interaction variable. This collinearity inflates the standard errors of the estimated regression coefficients, and it makes it impossible to get a unique sum of squares for each of the three explanatory variables. Centering the explanatory variables around their means reduces the collinearity, but this also may change the nature of the model. This point is discussed further in Chapter 4.

Ordinarily the estimated coefficients from the separate-equation method are different from the coefficients from the single-equation method. Limited experiences from Monte Carlo studies indicate that the coefficients from the single equation are usually closer to the true parameter values. Also, most often the As have smaller standard errors than the as, in spite of the collinearity that affects those standard errors. The main reason for the smaller standard errors is that the individual is the unit in that analysis, and the number of individuals is usually much larger than the number of groups, the unit in the separate-equation analysis.

The various residuals are related in the following way. If we substitute Equations 3.12 and 3.13 into Equation 3.11, we get

$$y_{ij} = d_{0j} + d_{1j} x_{ij} + f_{ij}$$

$$= (a_0 + a_2 \bar{x}_j + u_j) + (a_1 + a_3 \bar{x}_j + v_j) x_{ij} + f_{ij} \qquad [3.15]$$

$$= a_0 + a_1 x_{ij} + a_2 \bar{x}_j + a_3 x_{ij} \bar{x}_j + (f_{ij} + u_j + v_j x_{ij})$$

We know when we fit Y to the three effect variables in a multiple regression analysis of the form expressed in Equation 3.15 that the best fit with the smallest residual sum of squares is produced by the As. If we use any other set of coefficients, then the residual sum of squares will be larger. This means we have the following inequality,

$$\Sigma \Sigma e_{ij}^2 \leq \Sigma \Sigma (f_{ij} + u_j + v_j x_{ij})^2 \qquad [3.16]$$

Equality occurs only when the as are equal to the As.

Measuring Effects

Usually we are very interested in the question of how large the effects are on the dependent variable from the individual, group, and interaction variables. The forms of the effects can be seen in the signs and values of the regression coefficients for the three effects, but these coefficients do not tell us how large the effects are of the corresponding variables. The main reason for this is that the three variables are measured in different units.

A common way around that difficulty in multiple regression is to change the coefficients to standardized coefficients, and thereby compare how large the effects are of the different variables. It also is common in multiple regression to look at the sums of squares for the different explanatory variables as measures of the effects of the variables. The main difficulty with that approach is that when the variables themselves are correlated, there is no way of getting a unique sum of squares for each variable. What we can do is enter the variable in some specified order and look at the increase in the regression sum of squares from one step to the next. We may want to regress the dependent variable on the individual-level variable first and take that regression sum of squares as the measure of the magnitude of the effect of that variable. Next, we can enter the group variable and take the increase in the regression sum of squares as the measure of the effect of the group-level variable, after the individual variable has accounted for its effect. Finally, we can enter the interaction variable and take the corresponding increase in the regression sum of squares as the measure of the magnitude of the effect of that variable, after the individual and group variables have accounted for their effects.

Usually the variable entered first in a regression analysis gives the largest regression sum of squares. Often we are particularly interested in whether the individual or the group variable has the most effect, and if we enter the individual variable first it may well be the variable with the largest sum of squares. If we enter the group variable first, it may well be that this is the variable with the most effect. Thus, because of the correlation between the individual and group variables, we have no way of untangling the effects of these two variables. This problem of collinearity becomes less severe in the relative model and the centering method described below.

Another way to solve the problem of measuring effects is to take a closer look at the process we believe generated the data in the first place. This process is reflected in the model we work with in this chapter, and the model is shown in the various equations as well as in Figure 3.6. This figure shows the effects on a single observation of Y by the three effect variables and the residual variable.

The observation y_{ij} starts at α_0 when there are no effects present. When the observation is exposed to the individual-level variable, the effect of this variable is to move the observation up a distance $\alpha_1 x_{ij}$ up from α_0. This distance can be taken as the effect of the individual-level variable on that individual.

One way to think of the overall effect of the individual variable for all the individuals in the study is to add up all the distances the individuals were moved. That way the effect of the individual variable is measured as

$$\text{effect of individual variable} = |\alpha_1| \, \Sigma \, \Sigma \, | x_{ij} |.$$

We need the absolute value signs because we are only interested in how far the observations were moved, not whether they were moved up or down. When the values of X are all positive, the sum of the absolute values equals the number of observations times the mean of X. This is in contrast with simple regression or regression without collinearity, where the effect of a variable is measured by the sum of squares $\beta^2 \Sigma (x - \bar{x})^2$. One difference is that the distance an observation is moved because of X is measured from the overall mean to the regression line. Another difference is that the distances are squared before they are added up.

The presence of the group effect adds another $\alpha_2 \bar{x}_j$ to the value of Y. We see in Figure 3.6 how the group effect moves the observation up that additional distance. All the observations in the jth group have that amount added to their value of Y, and all the observations have been lifted the same distance. The effect of the group variable on all the observations in the jth group becomes $n_j \alpha_2 \bar{x}_j$. By adding these effects across all the groups we get the group variable effect as

$$\text{effect of group variable} = |\alpha_2| \, \Sigma \, n_j \, | \bar{x}_j | \, .$$

Again we need absolute values, because we are only interested in how far the observations were moved by the group variable, not whether they were moved up or down. When the X values are all positive or all negative, the sums are the same for the individual and group effects. In that case, the coefficients for those two variables can be compared directly to see which of the two variables has a larger effect.

The interaction variable adds the term $\alpha_3 x_{ij} \bar{x}_j$ to the value of Y for the ith person in the jth group. Therefore, the overall effect of the interaction variable can be taken as the sum of these effects to give us

$$\text{effect of interaction variable} = |\alpha_3| \, \Sigma \Sigma \, | x_{ij} \bar{x}_j | \, .$$

As before, we need the absolute values to find how far the interaction variable moves the points.

Finally, the residual variable moves the points off the lines to where we actually find the observations when we plot the observed data. In the spirit of thinking of effects as distances moved, the effect of the residual variable can be taken as the sum of the distances from the points to the within-group regression. That results in

$$\text{effect of residual variable} = \Sigma \Sigma \, | \varepsilon_{ij} | \, .$$

TABLE 3.3
Absolute Effects and Proportions of Effects for Each Variable

Source	Effect	Proportion
Individual	$\|\alpha_1\| \Sigma\Sigma\|x_{ij}\|$	P_{ind}
Group	$\|\alpha_2\| \Sigma n_j\|\bar{x}_j\|$	P_{gr}
Interaction	$\|\alpha_3\| \Sigma\Sigma\|x_{ij}\bar{x}_j\|$	P_{int}
Residual	$\Sigma\Sigma\|\varepsilon_{ij}\|$	P_{res}
Total	Sum	1.00

In the analysis of actual data we replace the parameters (alphas) with the estimated regression coefficients and the residuals (epsilons) by the observed residuals. In addition to these sums, the effect of each variable can be expressed as a proportion found by dividing the effect-sum for each variable by the sum of all four effect-sums.

These effects can be arranged in a table resembling the usual analysis-of-variance table, as seen in Table 3.3. The estimated effects are found by replacing the alphas with their estimates. The proportions in the last column are found by dividing each entry in the first column by the total in that column. This table has no columns for hypothesis testing, but we get a t value for each estimated regression coefficient, and they can be used to see if the corresponding effect is statistically significant.

Aggregate Data

There are times when we only have aggregate data available to us. Such aggregate data consist of the means of Y and X in each group, and there is no data available on individuals in the groups. Census data are often of this kind, where we may have means on two variables for a group of counties instead of the individual data that those means are based on. Election data also are most often of this kind, where we may have the percentage vote for a party and the percentage of people with a certain religious affiliation. For official election data the individual data are not even recorded, because they are generated in the privacy of the voting booth.

It is possible to study the relationships between such aggregate data, but the results we get apply only to the aggregate units and not to the people that make up the units. Trying to make the conclusions apply to individuals takes us directly into the ecological fallacy where we interpret results obtained on the group level as applicable to the individual level. As an example, we may find a relationship between the percentage of Catholics in a set of precincts and the percentage of Democratic votes. But this does not tell us, on the individual level, whether or not the Catholics are voting for the Democratic party.

To see what happens when we study the mean of Y as a function of the mean of X we can go back to Equation 3.10. There is an equation like that for each individual. If we add up the equations for all the individuals in a group and divide each side by the number of individuals in that group, we get the equation

$$\bar{y}_j = \alpha_0 + (\alpha_1 + \alpha_2)\,\bar{x}_j + \alpha_3\,\bar{x}_j^2 + \varepsilon_j \qquad [3.17]$$

The terms for the individual-level variable add up to their group sum, and when we divide by the number of observations in the group we get the group mean. Similarly, for the group-level variable we add up the group mean several times, and when we divide by the group size we get the group mean again. Thus, we can factor out the group mean, and we get the sum $(\alpha_1 + \alpha_2)$ as the coefficient for the group mean. Similarly, for the interaction-level variable we first get the sum of the X values times the group mean, and when we divide by the group size we get the group mean multiplied by itself. Finally, the mean of the residuals in the jth group is denoted ε_j.

From Equation 3.17 we see that when there is an interaction effect present, the relationship between the group means should be fitted with a second-order polynomial. In a scatterplot of the group means we should be able to see that the means are not linearly related. If there is no interaction effect present in our data then α_3 will equal zero, and in this special case the means will be linearly related.

When we regress the group mean of Y on the group mean of X as seen in Equation 3.17, the equation shows that we can get an estimate of the coefficient for the interaction variable. But the individual- and group-level coefficients will remain forever tangled. We can estimate their sum, but with only group data there is no way of breaking that sum up into separate estimates of the two coefficients. The only way we can hope to break them up is if we have any kind of additional

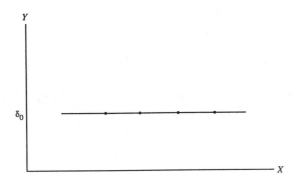

Figure 4.1. No Individual Effect Present for Four People

individual-level data. There may be survey data available on individuals within a few groups, for example.

4. CONTEXTUAL ANALYSIS WITH RELATIVE EFFECTS

In general, there is an individual-level effect of X present when two individuals in the same group who have different values of X also have different values of Y. In this chapter we use this same principle of individual-level effect to consider another contextual model called the *model with relative effects*. In the relative-effects model, the effects work in a different way from the absolute-effects model considered in Chapter 3.

As before, we start with the case where there are no effects present in the data. Without the individual effect present in a group, all persons in that group have the same value of Y irrespective of their value of X. This situation is illustrated in Figure 4.1 for a group with four individuals. Because their values of Y are equal, the four data points lie on a horizontal line. Let the intercept of this line be denoted by δ_0.

When we introduce an individual-level effect of X on Y, the data points within a group no longer lie on a horizontal line. If the relationship between the two variables is linear, then the points will lie on a line with nonzero slope. A major question becomes how the

36

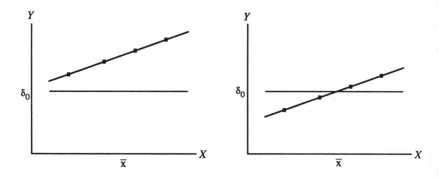

Figure 4.2. Absolute and Relative Individual Effects

points move off the horizontal line when the individual-level effect is introduced. One possibility is that the points move in such a way that the intercept for the new line is equal to the intercept of the old line. Another possibility is that the points move in such a way that the new line pivots around the mean point of the data. These two possibilities are shown in Figure 4.2.

In the plot on the left, the new line has the same intercept as the horizontal line where there are no effects. In this case, we say we have an *absolute individual effect,* the model discussed in Chapter 3. The new value of Y is a constant multiple of X, no matter what group the individual belongs to. As shown in Figure 3.3, there are groups to the left and the right of the group shown here, and the regression lines for the various groups lie along a straight line. The reason for the name *absolute* is that the absolute value of X determines the new value of Y.

In the plot on the right, the new line goes through the mean point of the data for this group. This pivoting of the regression line around the mean point implies that the effect of X is such that the points to the left of the group mean of X have moved down, and the points to the right of the mean have moved up. How far a point moves in this case depends on where the value of X is relative to the mean of X for the observations in the group. Therefore, the individual effect in this case is known as the *relative individual effect.*

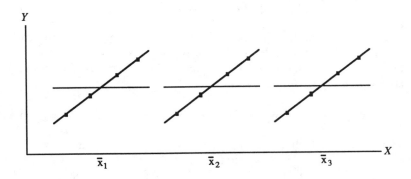

Figure 4.3. Relative Individual-Effect Model in Three Groups

Figure 4.3 illustrates the relative individual-effect model for three groups. This figure corresponds to Figure 3.3 for the absolute individual-effect model. As a possible example, let X be a person's age and Y the person's income. Figure 3.3 may be the case for three academic ranks. The full professors make more than the associate professors, who again make more than the assistant professors. But what really matters for the income is a person's age, and the graph shows that income goes up linearly with age. Figure 4.3 illustrates the same two variables, but suppose the first group consists of young lawyers, the second group consists of middle-aged doctors, and the third group consists of old professors. Any three people who are the same distance away from the mean age of their group here have the same income. What matters for the income is not the actual age, but age relative to the mean age of the group a person belongs to.

Mathematically, the line for the relationship between Y and X in the jth group can be expressed in the equation

$$y_{ij} = \delta_{0j} + \delta_{1j} x_{ij} + \varepsilon_{ij}.$$ [4.1]

For the relative model, it makes sense to subtract and add the term $\delta_{1j}\bar{x}_j$ on the right-hand side of the equation. In that case the equation can be rewritten in the form

$$y_{ij} = (\delta_{0j} + \delta_{1j}\bar{x}_j) + \delta_{1j}(x_{ij} - \bar{x}_j) + \varepsilon_{ij}. \qquad [4.2]$$

The sum within the first parentheses is a constant for the jth group, and it can be represented by the term μ_{0j}. Also, let $\delta_{1j} = \mu_{1j}$. With these changes Equation 4.2 for the relationship between the two variables can be written in the form

$$y_{ij} = \mu_{0j} + \mu_{1j}(x_{ij} - \bar{x}_j) + \varepsilon_{ij}. \qquad [4.3]$$

The difference from Chapter 3 is that for the relative model we subtract the group mean of X from each of the X values in the equation for the jth group. The slope of the regression line has not been changed, but the constant μ_0 now becomes the Y value when X is equal to the group mean, rather than when X is equal to zero.

Subtracting the group mean of X becomes more than just a technicality. It changes the model from an absolute to a relative model. Subtracting the group mean reflects the fact that the value of X for an individual relative to the mean of the group matters for the dependent variable, not simply for the value itself. Thus, with the relative model we study the effect of $X - \bar{X}_j$ on Y, whereas with the absolute model we study the effect of X itself on Y.

With J groups we have a set of J constants $\mu_{01}, \mu_{02}, \ldots, \mu_{0j}, \ldots, \mu_{0J}$ and a set of J slopes $\mu_{11}, \mu_{12}, \ldots, \mu_{1j}, \ldots, \mu_{1J}$. As for the absolute model, when the constants and slopes vary across the groups, then there must be something about the groups that affect the way X and Y are related within the different groups. We want to determine why the constants and slopes vary across the groups, and that can be expressed in the model equations

$$\text{constant } \mu_{0j} = \text{ function of something} \qquad [4.4]$$

$$\text{slope } \mu_{1j} = \text{ function of something.} \qquad [4.5]$$

Basic Model

The forms of these two equations and the functions that go into the equations are determined by the substantive issues being studied. One function, among many possible functions, is that the constants and slopes are both functions of the group means. The linear model with the group mean can be expressed in the model equations

$$\mu_{0j} = \beta_0 + \beta_2 (\bar{x}_j - \bar{x}) \qquad [4.6]$$

$$\mu_{1j} = \beta_1 + \beta_3 (\bar{x}_j - \bar{x}) . \qquad [4.7]$$

The model is expressed using four betas as parameters. The model equations look very much like the model equations we use for the absolute model. But for reasons discussed below we subtract the overall mean of X from the group means.

These are also deterministic models in the sense that there are no residual terms in the equations. But the mus and betas are all unknown parameters, and a deterministic model may well be appropriate. It is more important that we use the correct variables and equations for our model equations than whether we have deterministic or stochastic models. Residuals enter these equations when we replace the unknown mus on the left sides of the equations by the estimated constants and slopes obtained from the within-group regression analyses.

The four beta parameters in the model equations determine the presence of the various types of effects. There is no effect of $X - \bar{X}_j$ on Y when there is no relationship between X and Y within each group, and the regression lines for the various groups have the same intercepts. In that case we have a set of horizontal within-group regression lines with common intercepts, as shown in Figure 3.2. In this case $\beta_1 = \beta_3 = 0$, because the regression lines are all horizontal and have slopes equal to zero. Also, $\beta_2 = 0$ because all the regression lines have the same intercept.

When we substitute the model equations with these parameter values back into Equation 4.3 for the within-group relationship, we get the equation

$$y_{ij} = \beta_0 + \varepsilon_{ij} . \qquad [4.8]$$

This says that the regression lines within all the groups are horizontal and have the same intercept β_0.

Let us now introduce the relative individual effect. With that effect it matters for the values of Y what the values of X are relative to the group mean of X. Without the presence of a group effect it does not matter what group a person belongs to. The relative individual effect works such that all individuals who are located a certain distance from the group mean, whatever the group, will have the same value of Y aside from the residual effect. This case is illustrated in Figure 4.3.

The within-group regression lines in Figure 4.3 all have the same constants and slopes. Using the model equations in Equations 4.6 and 4.7 we see that in this case $\beta_2 = \beta_3 = 0$, because the constants and slopes are not affected by the group means. When we substitute the model equations with these parameter values back into Equation 4.3 we get the equation

$$y_{ij} = \beta_0 + \beta_1 (x_{ij} - \overline{x}_j) + \varepsilon_{ij}. \qquad [4.9]$$

This equation says that all the lines have the same slope, and when X is equal to the group mean, Y is equal to the common value β_0 no matter what group the individual belongs to, plus a residual term. The level of Y is the same in each group. The individual effect is represented by the parameter β_1.

It can be shown in this case of the relative individual effect that the estimate of the parameter β_1 becomes the mean of the estimated slopes within the groups. Because the model specifies that the groups have the same slope, it is not surprising that the best estimate of this common slope is the mean of the within-group slopes.

It also is possible to illustrate this case in a slightly different way. The values of the independent variable are found by subtracting the group mean from every observation. Within each group the mean of these new observations is therefore equal to 0. All observations smaller than the mean in the various groups have negative differences, and the observations larger than the mean in the various groups have positive differences. This way the groups will be superimposed and all the within-group lines will be superimposed as well, because they now have the same intercepts and slopes. This is illustrated in Figure 4.4, which takes the three lines in Figure 4.3 and superimposes them so that we only see one line.

This figure shows again that what matters for Y is where the value of X is relative to the group mean. Two individuals in different groups but with the same distance to the group mean have the same predicted value of Y. This relative feature of the model distinguishes the relative model from the absolute model. We also see that there is

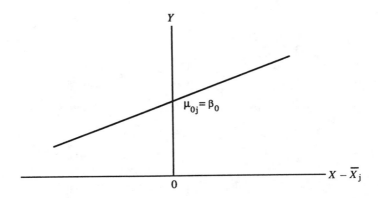

Figure 4.4. Superimposed Lines in Relative Model

no group effect present here, because it only matters for an individual what the relative value of X is to determine the value of Y.

There is a group effect present only when there is no relationship between X and Y within the groups and the groups have different intercepts. This case is already illustrated in Figure 3.4 with horizontal within-group lines and the lines at different heights. Because the lines have zero slopes, it follows from the model equations that we must have $\beta_1 = \beta_3 = 0$. Because the intercepts are different we have $\beta_2 \neq 0$. Thus, β_2 becomes the parameter for the group effect.

When we use these parameter values and substitute the model equations back into Equation 4.3 for the within-group relationship, we get the equation

$$y_{ij} = \beta_0 + \beta_2 \, (\bar{x}_j - \bar{x}) + \varepsilon_{ij} . \qquad [4.10]$$

This says that aside from the residuals, all values of Y in group j are equal. Within each group, X is not related to Y. But it makes a difference for Y what group a person belongs to, and we express that by saying that there is a group effect of X on Y.

When we regress Y on the group means as expressed in Equation 4.10, it can be shown that the estimate of the group effect coefficient β_2 is the slope of the line that best fits the points with coordinates $(\bar{x}_j, \bar{y}_j)$. These points are the points for the group means.

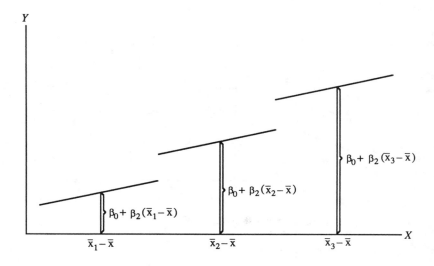

Figure 4.5. Relative Individual and Group Effects

There are both individual and group effects present when the within-group lines have the same nonzero slope and different constants. This case is illustrated in Figure 4.5. Because the slopes are equal, we see from the model equations that we must have $\beta_3 = 0$. Similarly, because the slopes are different from 0, we must have $\beta_1 \neq 0$. Finally, because the constants are different and there is a group effect present, we must have $\beta_2 \neq 0$. The final parameter β_0 may or may not be equal to 0. Without a group effect the lines would have had the same height above the X axis. Without an individual effect the lines would have pivoted around the center point to a horizontal position.

It is possible to substitute the model equations for this case where the model parameter $\beta_3 = 0$ into the within-group relationship expressed in Equation 4.3. When there is both an individual and a group effect present we get the equation

$$y_{ij} = \beta_0 + \beta_1 (x_{ij} - \overline{x}_j) + \beta_2 (\overline{x}_j - \overline{x}) + \varepsilon_{ij}. \qquad [4.11]$$

A scatterplot of Y versus X with within-group regression lines will look like the lines in Figure 4.5. From Equation 4.11 we see that we

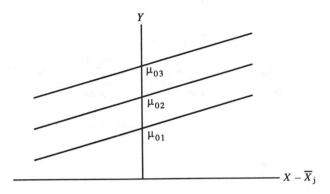

Figure 4.6. Individual and Group Effects

use the difference between an observation and the group mean as one of the independent variables. When we plot Y against that variable, we get the set of lines shown in Figure 4.6. The lines are all centered around the value of 0 on the horizontal axis, and the lines stack up above each other. We see the presence of the individual effect because the lines have nonzero slopes, and we see the presence of the group effect because the intercepts are different.

Finally, there is an individual-group interaction effect present when the parameter $\beta_3 \neq 0$. In that case the within-group slope depends on the group mean of X, and then the lines will have different slopes.

Thus, it is the interaction effect that produces the different slopes. When the full model equations are substituted into the equation for the within group relationship, we get the equation

$$y_{ij} = \beta_0 + \beta_1 (x_{ij} - \overline{x}_j) + \beta_2 (\overline{x}_j - \overline{x}) + \beta_3 (x_{ij} - \overline{x}_j)(\overline{x}_j - \overline{x}) + \varepsilon_{ij}. \quad [4.12]$$

This equation shows how the observed value of Y is related to position of the person's value on X relative to the group mean, the mean of the group the person belongs to relative to the overall mean, and to the product of these two factors.

These effects also are illustrated in Figure 4.7. The figure shows how the observed value of Y is built up as a sum of different effects. Without any effects the data points would be on the horizontal line.

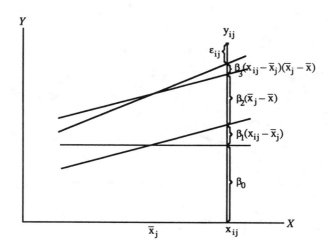

Figure 4.7. Relative Individual, Group, and Interaction Effects on Y

The individual effect pivots the line around the mean point. The group effect moves the line up, and the interaction effect pivots the line again.

The effects in Figure 4.7 can be compared with the absolute effects in Figure 3.6. The data points look the same in these two cases, but the data have been generated by two very different processes. Because the data look the same in the two cases, there is no way to differentiate between the absolute and the relative model on the basis of the data alone. This is a choice that must be made on a substantive basis. When both models are applied to the same data, we get very different measures of the forms and magnitudes of the three effects.

Estimation of Parameters

There are two sets of parameters to estimate in the relative model, just as there are two sets in the absolute model. First, there are the mus used to characterize the relationship between X and Y within each group. Those parameters also are used as dependent variables in the model equations. Second, there are the betas used to model the way in which the mus are determined. In the special case we discuss here, the betas are the coefficients in the linear equations with the group mean as the independent variable.

The mus can be estimated by regressing Y on X within each group. For the jth group we get the estimated relationship between Y and X expressed in the equation

$$y_{ij} = m_{0j} + m_{1j} (x_{ij} - \bar{x}_j) + f_{ij} \qquad [4.13]$$

where the fs are the estimated residuals. From these analyses we get one constant and one slope for each group. The constant equals the group mean of Y; that is, $m_{0j} = \bar{y}_j$.

These estimated constants and slopes do not tell us anything directly about the existence of individual, group, and interaction effects. But to the extent that these regression coefficients differ from group to group, we know that there are possible effects present in the data. Therefore, it is always important, as a first step, to examine the relationship between Y and X within the groups and see if constants and slopes differ from group to group.

There are two main ways in which the effect parameters (betas) can be estimated. The first uses the group as the unit in the analysis, and this method is the separate-equations method. The second uses the individual as the unit, and this is the single-equation method.

The separate-equations method is based on the two model equations (4.6 and 4.7). We do not have the actual mus on the left sides of those equations, but we have estimated mus from the regression analyses within the groups, and we use those estimated mus instead of the true mus. The difference between the true and the estimated mus becomes the residual in a regression analysis that can be used to estimate the betas.

By regressing the observed constants and slopes on the group means, we get the following two estimated model equations,

$$m_{0j} = b_0 + b_2 (\bar{x}_j - \bar{x}) + u_j \qquad [4.14]$$

$$m_{1j} = b_1 + b_3 (\bar{x}_j - \bar{x}) + v_j \qquad [4.15]$$

where the us and the vs are the estimated residuals and the bs are the estimated betas.

The unit in these two analyses is the group. Therefore, this method may not be a good way to estimate the betas if we only have a small number of groups. The small number of data points will tend to make the standard errors of the coefficients large. When the number of individuals varies a great deal across the groups, it is better to weigh the size of the group in the analysis. That way the larger groups will count more than the smaller groups. With a weighted regression the coefficient b_0 becomes equal to the overall mean of Y, and the coefficient b_1 becomes the average within-group slope.

The single-equation method is based on Equation 4.12. This equation shows that when we have a linear relationship between Y and X within the groups and the group constants and slopes are functions of the group means, the value of Y for an individual is a function of the individual's value of X minus the group mean, the group mean minus the overall mean, and the product of these two variables.

This equation can be used to estimate the betas. To perform this regression analysis, some recoding of the original data on X must be performed. We have to construct one individual-level column consisting of the differences between the original values of X and the group means of X. A second group-level column has to have the difference between the group means and the overall mean, with one such number for each individual in the study. The third individual-group interaction column consists of the product of the two previous columns.

Regressing Y on the individual, group, and interaction variables results in the estimated regression equation

$$y_{ij} = B_0 + B_1 (x_{ij} - \bar{x}_j) + B_2 (\bar{x}_j - \bar{x}) + B_3 (x_{ij} - \bar{x}_j)(\bar{x}_j - \bar{x}) + e_{ij} \quad [4.16]$$

where the Bs are the estimated regression coefficients and the es are the estimated residuals. The estimated coefficients from the single-equation method are denoted by capital Bs to distinguish these estimates from the bs obtained from the separate-equations method.

This relative model does not have the same problems with collinearity as the absolute model has. The three explanatory variables in Equation 4.16 have in most cases very few or no intercorrelations. When the three variables are uncorrelated, the estimated coefficients from the separate equations and from the single equation are equal. The coefficients from the single equation have smaller standard errors because the estimation is based on a larger number of data points.

Analysis of Relative Residuals

Because of the balanced nature of the variables in the single equation, it is possible to analyze the residuals in the relative model in a way that is not possible in the absolute model.

If we substitute Equations 4.14 and 4.15 into Equation 4.13, we get the equation

$$y_{ij} = m_{0j} + m_{1j}(x_{ij} - \overline{x}_j) + f_{ij}$$

$$= (b_0 + b_2(\overline{x}_j - \overline{x}) + u_j) + (b_1 + b_3(\overline{x}_j - \overline{x}) + v_j)(x_{ij} - \overline{x}_j) + f_{ij}$$

$$= b_0 + b_1(x_{ij} - \overline{x}_j) + b_2(\overline{x}_j - \overline{x}) + b_3(x_{ij} - \overline{x}_j)(\overline{x}_j - \overline{x}) \qquad [4.17]$$

$$+ (f_{ij} + u_j + v_j(x_{ij} - \overline{x}_j)).$$

When the bs are equal to the Bs, which they most often are in the case of the relative model, we see from Equations 4.16 and 4.17 that e_{ij} is equal to the last term in Equation 4.17. That is,

$$e_{ij} = f_{ij} + u_j + v_j(x_{ij} - \overline{x}_j). \qquad [4.18]$$

When we square the two sides of this equation and add the squares across all the observations, we get the equality

$$\Sigma\Sigma e_{ij}^2 = \Sigma\Sigma f_{ij}^2 + \Sigma n_j u_j^2 + \Sigma\Sigma (v_j(x_{ij} - \overline{x}_j))^2. \qquad [4.19]$$

The square of the right-hand side of Equation 4.18 involves all three possible cross products in addition to the squares. But it can be shown that the three sums of the cross products equal zero. This means we have partitioned the residual sum of square from the single equation into three components.

The sum of the e squares measures the unexplained variation in Y due to all variables other than the individual, group, and interaction effects of the X variable. Thus, this sum of squares measures the unexplained variation in Y due to the individual, group, and interaction effects of all variables other than X. In Equation 4.19 the unexplained variation in Y is partitioned into three components.

The first component is the sum of the f squares. This sum comes from the analyses of the relationship between Y and X within the groups. The sum of the f squares becomes the unexplained variation in Y due to all individual-level variables other than X. The second and the third components come from the regression analyses of the model equations. The sum of the u squares measures the unexplained variation due to all group-level variables other than X. Similarly, the third sum of squares measures the unexplained variation due to all interaction variables other than X.

Thus, in the relative model we are able to partition the unexplained variation in Y into components that can be thought of as the unexplained parts of the individual, group, and interaction variables other than X.

Measuring Effects

As with the absolute effects model, we are usually interested in how large the effects are on the dependent variable of the individual, group, and interaction variables. The forms of the effects can be seen in the signs and values of the estimated regression coefficients for the three effects. But the coefficients themselves do not tell us how large the effects are of the corresponding variables. The main reason for this is that the variables are measured in different units.

One way around that problem is to change the coefficients to standardized regression coefficients and compare those coefficients. It also is possible to partition the regression sum of squares into components due to each of the three variables. With uncorrelated individual, group, and interaction variables in the relative model, this becomes a particularly attractive way of studying the effects of the three variables. When the three variables are uncorrelated, we get unique component sums of squares for the three variables.

We find the regression sum of squares for the individual variable by regressing Y on the first explanatory variable in Equation 4.16. This gives the following sum of squares measuring the effect on Y by the individual-level effect of X on Y:

$$\text{Individual-level effect} = b_1^2 \, \Sigma \, \Sigma \, (x_{ij} - \bar{x}_j)^2 \, .$$

Similarly, the regression sum of square for the group variable is found by regressing Y on the second explanatory variable in Equation 4.16. This gives the following sum of squares measuring the effect on Y by the group-level effect of X:

TABLE 4.1
Sums of Squares for Various Effects

Effect	Explained	Unexplained	Total
Individual	$b_1^2 \Sigma\Sigma (x_{ij} - \overline{x}_j)^2$	$\Sigma\Sigma f_{ij}^2$	Sum_{ind}
Group	$b_2^2 \Sigma n_j (\overline{x}_j - \overline{x})^2$	$\Sigma n_j u_i^2$	Sum_{gr}
Interaction	$b_3^2 \Sigma\Sigma [(x_{ij} - \overline{x}_j)(\overline{x}_j - \overline{x})]^2$	$\Sigma\Sigma [v_j (x_{ij} - \overline{x}_j)]^2$	Sum_{int}
Total	Regressive sum of squares	$\Sigma\Sigma e_{ij}^2$	$\Sigma\Sigma (y_{ij} - \overline{y})^2$

$$\text{Group-level effect} = b_2^2 \Sigma n_j (\overline{x}_j - \overline{x})^2 .$$

Finally, the interaction effect is found by regressing Y on the third explanatory variable in Equation 4.16. This gives the interaction-level effect of X on Y:

$$\text{Interaction-level effect} = b_3^2 \Sigma\Sigma [(x_{ij} - \overline{x}_j)(\overline{x}_j - \overline{x})]^2 .$$

We now have both explained and unexplained variations of the individual-, group-, and interaction-level variables. These effects can be arranged in an extended analysis-of-variance table, as seen in Table 4.1.

It also is possible to divide each entry by the total sum of squares in the lower right corner of the table. That gives us a table showing the various sums of squares as proportions (or percentages) of the total, and such a table may be easier to read. The numbers in the total column tell us how much of the overall variation in the dependent variable is due to all individual-, group-, and interaction-level variables. Similarly, the first column shows the variation in Y explained by the individual, group, and interaction effects of X. The second column divides the unexplained variation in Y into effects due to all other individual, group, and interaction variables.

The rows show how much of the variation in Y is explained by X, and how much is explained by other variables, for each of the three kinds of explanatory variables as well as for the total effect. Taken together, the rows and columns of the table may show a variety of patterns. It may be, for example, that the individual-level effect of X is higher than the group and interaction effects. At the same time, it may be that the group effect shows a proportionally higher unexplained effect than does the individual-level effect. Such a table may show us where we should search if we are looking for variables we can introduce to cut down on the unexplained variation in Y.

There is also another way of looking at how large the effects are of the explanatory variables on the dependent variable. There was a certain process that produced the observed values of Y. An individual is exposed to individual, group, and interaction effects, and this exposure generates the observed value of Y. We try to represent this process in our model, and with the relative effect model we think the process is the one that is illustrated in Figure 4.7.

An individual starts with the value of Y being equal to β_0. When this individual is exposed to the effect of the individual-level variable, the result is that the value $\beta_1(x_{ij} - \bar{x}_j)$ is added to the original value of β_0. This distance can be taken as the effect of the individual-level variable on that individual. One way to think of the overall effect of the individual-level variable for all the individuals in the study is to add up all the distances the individuals were moved. That way the effect of the individual level variable is measured by the sum

$$\text{effect of individual variable} = |\beta_1| \, \Sigma \, \Sigma \, |x_{ij} - \bar{x}_j| \, .$$

We need the absolute-value signs because we are only interested in how far the observations were moved, not whether they were moved up or down. Also, without the absolute values for the terms involving the xs, that sum would be zero. By taking absolute values we give the same weight to all distances, whereas squaring gives proportionally more weight to larger distances than smaller ones.

From Figure 4.7 we see that exposing this person to the group variable adds an additional $\beta_2(\bar{x}_j - \bar{x})$ to the value of Y. All the observations in the jth group have that amount added to their value of Y, and all the observations are lifted by that distance. Adding these distances for the observations in the jth group gives a total distance of $n_j\beta_2(\bar{x}_j - \bar{x})$. By adding these effects across all the groups we get the group-variable effect as the sum

$$\text{effect of group variable} = |\beta_2| \, \Sigma \, n_j \, |\bar{x}_j - \bar{x}| \, .$$

Again, we need absolute values because we are only interested in how far the observations were moved by the group variable, not whether they were moved up or down.

TABLE 4.2
Relative Effects and Proportions of Effects for Each Variable

Source	Effect	Proportion
Individual	$\|\beta_1\| \Sigma\Sigma \|x_{ij} - \bar{x}_j\|$	P_{ind}
Group	$\|\beta_2\| \Sigma n_j \|\bar{x}_j - \bar{x}\|$	P_{gr}
Interaction	$\|\beta_3\| \Sigma\Sigma \|(x_{ij} - \bar{x}_j)(\bar{x}_j - \bar{x})\|$	P_{int}
Residual	$\Sigma\Sigma \|\varepsilon_{ij}\|$	P_{res}
Total	Sum	1.00

The interaction term $\beta_3(x_{ij} - \bar{x}_j)(\bar{x}_j - \bar{x})$ is added as the effect of the interaction variable for the ith person in the jth group. Therefore, the overall effect of the interaction variable can be taken as the sum of these effects, to give us

$$\text{effect of the interaction variable} = |\beta_3| \Sigma\Sigma |(x_{ij} - \bar{x}_j)(\bar{x}_j - \bar{x})|.$$

As before, we need absolute values to find how far the interaction variable moves the points.

Finally, we see from Figure 4.7 that it is the residual variable that pushes the ith observation in the jth group off the regression line to where we actually observe that value of Y. The effect of the residual variable on that observation is denoted ε_{ij}. The total distance the residual variable pushes the observations can be measured by the sum of the absolute values of the residual. We take this sum to measure the effect of the residual variable for the entire set of observations. Thus,

$$\text{effect of the residual variable} = \Sigma\Sigma |\varepsilon_{ij}|.$$

These effects can be summarized in a table similar to Table 3.3. Table 4.2 resembles the usual analysis-of-variance table, except that there are sums of absolute values instead of sums of squares.

The estimated effects are found by replacing the betas by their estimates. The proportions in the last column are found by dividing each entry in the first column by the total in that column. This table has no columns for hypothesis testing, but we get a t value for each estimated regression coefficient, and the t values can be used to see if the corresponding effect is statistically significant.

Aggregate Data

There are times when we only have aggregate data available. For the dependent variable we have the mean $\bar{y}_j$ in the jth group and for the independent variable we have the mean $\bar{x}_j$. Census data are often of this kind, where we may have means for counties instead of data on individuals. Election data are also of this kind, where we may have the percentage vote for a party and the percentage of people with a certain religious affiliation.

It is possible to study the relationship between such aggregate variables, but the results we get only apply to the aggregate units and not to the individuals that make up the units. Trying to make the conclusions apply to the individuals takes us directly into the ecological fallacy, where we erroneously interpret results obtained on the group level to apply to the individual level.

To see what happens when we regress the mean of Y on the mean of X we can go back to Equation 4.12. There is an equation like that for each individual. If we add up the equations for all the individuals in a group and divide each side by the number of individuals in that group, we get the equation

$$\bar{y}_j = \beta_0 + \beta_2 (\bar{x}_j - \bar{x}) + \varepsilon_j .\qquad [4.20]$$

The terms for the individual effect add up to zero, and we get no variable for the individual effect parameter β_1. The same thing happens for the interaction variable, and we get no variable for the interaction-effect parameter β_3. The mean of the residuals in the jth group is denoted ε_j.

Equation 4.20 is the same as the first model equation shown in Equation 4.14, because the constant m_{0j} is the same as the mean of Y in the jth group. That can be seen from Equation 4.13.

From Equation 4.20 we see that we can get an estimate of the group effect parameter β_2, but that is all. From the form of Equation 4.20 we see that the slope b_2 is the slope of the line that best fits the mean points with coordinates $(\bar{x}_j, \bar{y}_j)$. Thus, if these mean points do not fall along a straight line, that is a sign that this is not the appropriate model to work with.

There is no reason to believe that the estimate b_2 can be used as an estimate of the individual-level parameter β_1. Thus, group data alone cannot be used to draw conclusions about individual-level effects. For this model the single-equation regression equation reduces to the first model equation when we have aggregate data only. We have no way of getting the within-group slopes in this case, and therefore it is not possible to estimate the individual-level coefficient b_1 and the interaction-level coefficient b_3.

Absolute Versus Relative Model

Initially there does not seem to be any observable feature of our data that can guide us in the choice of whether we should use the absolute or the relative model. In principle, this choice of whether it is X or $X - \overline{X}_j$ that influences Y should be made on substantive grounds. We should know enough about the process that generated the data in the first place to make the choice between the two models. In both cases the data give us a set of within-group regression lines, and these data can be analyzed by both models. The results of the two analyses usually will be different, and it becomes important for our conclusions which model we choose.

The sections on aggregate data in Chapters 3 and 4 show that there is a way of using the data to choose between the two models. Equations 3.16 and 4.20 show the relationship between the group means of Y and X. From Equation 3.16 we see that for the absolute model the relationship between the group means is nonlinear in the case when there is an interaction effect present. From Equation 4.20 we see that for the relative model the relationship between the group means is always linear.

This distinction helps us use the data to choose between the two models. If the relationship between the group means of Y and X is nonlinear and can be fitted using a squared term, then we have data from the absolute model. If the relationship between the means is linear, then we either have data generated by the relative model or we have data from the absolute model in a case without any interaction effect. This rule does not provide us with a sure method to choose between the two models, but the rule can be helpful in making the choice.

5. EXAMPLES OF ABSOLUTE AND RELATIVE DATA

The Data and Choice of Models

In this chapter we illustrate some of the computations that are discussed in the two previous chapters. Table 5.1 shows two sets of Y values while the X variable is the same for the two data sets. These two sets of Y values have been generated with known parameter values, giving us an opportunity to see how well the various estimation procedures work. The first column of Y values has been generated according to an absolute model, and the second column has been generated by a relative model.

The table contains data with five observations in each of five groups. The groups are separated by blank lines. In a regular data matrix there would be another column used to identify the groups. From the observed data we have to generate several new columns to analyze the data. For the absolute model we need one column of group means for the X variable, such that the first five observations would have a value of 3 on this variable, the next five would have a value of 4, and so on. Finally, we need a column that is the product of the original X values and the group means. The first few values of this interaction variable become 3, 6, 9, and so on.

For the relative model we need to construct an individual-level variable by subtracting the group mean from each of the observations of X. For all groups these values become -2, -1, 0, 1, 2. Next, the group effect variable is the difference between the group mean and the overall mean. Thus, the values of this variable for the first five observations become -2, the next five observations will have -1, and so on. The interaction variable is constructed as the product of the individual and group variables. The first few values of this variable become 4, 2, 0, -2, -4, 2, 1, and so on.

Most of the time we do not know whether the data have been generated according to the absolute or the relative model. From Equations 3.16 and 4.20 we see that when there is an interaction effect present in the data, then data generated by the absolute model give us a curvilinear relationship between the group means. Data generated by the relative model give us a linear relationship between the group means. Therefore, as a first step in the analysis we make a scatterplot of the group means and analyze these group means to see whether they are related in a linear or nonlinear fashion.

TABLE 5.1
Two Sets of Y Values and Their X Values

Y Absolute Effects	Y Relative Effects	X Variable
27	1.1	1
40	5.2	2
58	15.1	3
63	17.0	4
82	17.8	5
35	1.1	2
53	7.5	3
55	16.4	4
77	21.0	5
80	30.2	6
51	11.7	3
59	5.8	4
64	20.2	5
67	28.6	6
79	40.0	7
57	4.0	4
54	7.5	5
57	26.8	6
64	38.1	7
65	48.4	8
49	4.0	5
48	13.4	6
53	29.8	7
54	45.7	8
55	60.2	9

Figure 5.1 shows the scatterplots of the group means for the two sets of Y values. The plot on the left shows the Y values from the first column for the absolute data, and the plot on the right shows the Y values from the second column for the relative model. The five points in the scatterplots represent the five groups of data. The scatterplots also show the regression line that best fits the data. The pattern of the points in the left plot is such that it seems as if the points could be well fitted by an equation with an xbar-squared variable. This is the equation for a parabola, and the five points look as if they could be

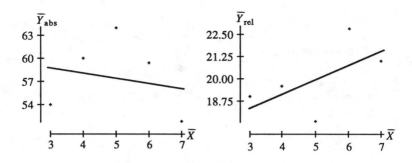

Figure 5.1. Scatterplots and Regression Lines for Group Means, for the Data in Table 5.1

well fitted by such a curve. A regression analysis of the means of Y on the means of X and the square of the means of X shows a highly significant coefficient for the xbar-squared variable. The points in the right scatterplot show more of a linear trend. An analysis of the relationship in those points gives a very insignificant coefficient for the square of xbar. This leads us to choose the absolute model for the first set of Y values and the relative model for the second set of Y values.

Analysis of the Absolute Data

The data in the first column of Table 5.1 were generated according to the absolute model with normal random residuals and the following parameter values:

$$\alpha_0 = 0.0 \quad \alpha_1 = 20.0 \quad \alpha_2 = 5.0 \quad \alpha_3 = -2.5$$

The first step in a contextual analysis consists of regressing Y on X within each of the groups to get the intercepts and slopes. These analyses give the following results:

Group	d_0	d_1
1	$\hat{y} = 14.1 + 13.3x$	

$$2 \qquad \hat{y} = 14.4 + 11.4x$$

$$3 \qquad \hat{y} = 32.0 + 6.4x$$

$$4 \qquad \hat{y} = 43.8 + 2.6x$$

$$5 \qquad \hat{y} = 39.2 + 1.8x$$

Here is a case where the intercepts and slopes vary a great deal across the five groups, and this is an indication that group memberships should be considered for us to understand more fully the relationship between Y and X.

In the rest of this section we use the model that specifies that the group intercepts and slopes are linear functions of the group means of X. The group mean of X is only one of many possible variables that could be used to explain why the groups have different intercepts and slopes. To estimate the parameters we first use the separate-equations method and then the single-equation method.

For the separate-equations method we regress the observed intercepts and slopes on the group means of X. This gives us the estimates of the effect parameters with their standard errors in parentheses as shown below:

$$d_{0j} = -11.1 + 7.96\bar{x}_j + u_j \qquad d_{1j} = 23.0 - 3.18\bar{x}_j + v_j \qquad [5.1]$$
$$\quad (10.95) \ (2.11) \qquad\qquad\quad (2.04) \ (0.39)$$

The coefficient $a_1 = 23.0$ shows that there is an individual level effect of X present in these data. The coefficient $a_2 = 7.96$ shows that there is a group level effect of X present, and the coefficient $a_3 = -3.18$ shows that there is an individual-group interaction effect present as well. From the magnitudes of the standard errors we see that all three coefficients are well beyond two standard deviations from 0, and therefore they are highly significantly different from zero. We also see that each of the four estimates are within two standard errors of the true parameter values.

For the single-equation method we regress Y on the individual, group, and interaction variables. This analysis results in the equation

$$y_{ij} = -6.90 + 21.72x_{ij} + 7.02\bar{x}_j - 2.92x_{ij}\bar{x}_j + f_{ij}. \qquad [5.2]$$
$$\quad (6.58) \quad (1.41) \qquad (1.49) \qquad (0.26)$$

58

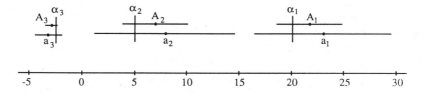

Figure 5.2. True and Estimated Parameter Values, with 95% Confidence Intervals

The standard errors are shown in parentheses below the coefficients. The coefficient $A_1 = 21.72$ shows that there is an individual-level effect of X present in these data. The coefficient $A_2 = 7.02$ shows that there is a group-level effect of X present, and the coefficient $A_3 = -2.92$ shows that there is an individual-group interaction effect present as well. All three coefficients are significantly different from zero. We also see that each of the four estimates is within two standard errors of the true parameter values.

When we compare the estimates from the separate equations in Equation 5.1 with the estimates from the single equation in Equation 5.2, we see that the single-equation estimates are all closer to the true parameter values than the separate-equations estimates. Also, the standard errors for the estimates from the single equation are all smaller than the standard errors from the separate-equation estimates.

The estimates and their standard errors are illustrated in Figure 5.2. The figure shows the true values of the three effect parameters, marked by vertical lines. The estimates from the separate equations are shown as as and the estimates from the single equation are shown as As. For each estimate there is a corresponding 95% confidence interval. We see that each of the six confidence intervals contains the corresponding true parameter value. Also, all the As are closer to the true values than the as are. Finally, the confidence intervals for the As are shorter than the confidence intervals for the as.

There are two reasons for that. One reason is that the As have smaller standard errors than the as, mainly because the As come from one multiple regression analysis based on as many as 25 observations, and the as come from simple regression analyses based on only 5 observations each. The second reason for the shorter intervals is that the

TABLE 5.2
Sequential Regression Sums of Squares

Variable	Sum of Squares	Proportion
Individual	1,089	0.26
Group, after individual	613	0.14
Interaction, after individual, group	2,284	0.54
Residual	249	0.06
Total	4,235	1.00

values of the t variable used as multiples for the confidence intervals are smaller for the As than for the as. This is again due to the different number of data points in the two types of analyses. For the As we use a value of t with 21 degrees of freedom, and for the as we use a value of t with only 3 degrees of freedom.

Next, we want to assess how large the effects of the three explanatory variables on Y are. This is problematic here because of the high intercorrelations between the individual, group, and interaction variables. In this example, the variables are so highly correlated that it makes little sense to compare the magnitudes of the standardized regression coefficients.

One thing we can do is to partition the regression sum of squares into three components. There is no unique way of doing that because the three effect variables are so highly correlated. But we can regress the variables in some order and measure the increases in the regression sum of squares. Table 5.2 shows the various regression sums of squares.

By regressing Y on the individual-level variable we get a regression sum of squares of 1,089. Regressing Y on both the individual- and the group-level variable gives a regression sum of squares of 1,702. This means that the group variable increased the regression sum of squares by $1,702 - 1,089 = 613$, and we take that to be the group sum of squares that measures the effect of the group variable. To find the interaction sum of squares, we regress Y on all three variables and find the increase in the regression sum of squares due to the addition of the interaction variables. From the numbers in Table 5.2 we see that the interaction variable seems to have a large effect, even if it is entered last in the analysis. This may be somewhat misleading; when the interaction variable is entered first it only produces a sum of

TABLE 5.3
True and Estimated Effects, Based on Sums of Absolute Values

| | Estimated | | True | |
Source	Effect	Proportion	Effect	Proportion
Individual	2,715	0.48	2,500	0.51
Group	878	0.16	625	0.13
Interaction	1,971	0.35	1,688	0.35
Residual	64	0.01	70	0.01
Total	5,428	1.00	4,883	1.00

squares equal to 165. It also is possible to enter the group variable first and let the subsequent increases in the regression sum of squares measure effects of the individual and interaction variables.

From sums of squares we turn to sums of absolute values, as displayed in Table 3.3. This approach removes the ambiguity we have with the sums of squares of what sequence the variables should be entered into the analysis. The expressions in Table 3.3 for the effects contain the actual parameter values. When we substitute the estimates we get from the single-equation estimation, we get the effects shown in Table 5.3. Because we know the true values of the parameters, we also can find the true values of the effects based on sums of absolute values. Table 5.3 contains these true effects as well as the proportions of effects due to the different variables. It also would be possible to use the estimated parameter values we obtained from the two separate equations, but the results are not very different from the estimated effects shown in the table.

We see that the estimated and true proportions of effects are very close to each other, meaning that the estimation procedure works well. It is not surprising that the estimated effect of the residual variable is a little smaller than the true effect, because the parameters are estimated trying to make the estimated residuals as small as possible.

Using the sum of absolute values we find that in these data the individual-effect variable is the most important, followed by the interaction variable. There is only a small group effect in these data. From the given values of the effect parameters, it is expected that the interaction variable will have a large effect. For example, if we chose one particular individual, say the fourth individual in the fourth group, we have the following relationship between the dependent variable and the three explanatory variables:

$$y_{44} = 0 + 20\,x_{44} + 5\,\bar{x}_4 - 2.5\,x_{44}\,\bar{x}_4 + \varepsilon_{44}$$

$$64 = 0 + 20*7 + 5*6 - 2.5*7*6 - 1 \qquad\qquad [5.3]$$

$$64 = 0 + 140 + 30 - 105 - 1$$

This person starts with a value of 0 when there are no effects present, and after this individual has been exposed to the individual, group, interaction, and residual effects, the person ends up with the observed value of 64. The individual-level variable adds 140, the group-level variable adds another 30, the interaction variable subtracts 105, and the residual variable subtracts another 1. For this person, the individual and the interaction variables have large effects. The individual variable contributes 140 to the overall individual effect of 2,500 for all the observations, and the interaction variable contributes 105 to the overall interaction effect of 1,688. Similar computations can be made for the other 24 observations.

The results using sums of squares are shown in Table 5.2. A comparison of the various results shows that the sums of squares overestimate the effect of the interaction and residual variables on the expense of the individual-level variable.

Analysis of the Relative Data

The data in the second column in Table 5.1 were generated according to the relative model with normal random residuals and the following parameter values:

$$\beta_0 = 20.0 \qquad \beta_1 = 10.0 \qquad \beta_2 = 5.0 \qquad \beta_3 = 2.5$$

The first step in the analysis of these data consists of regressing Y on X within each of the five groups to get the constants and the slopes. We know that these data have been generated by the relative model, and we could see from the scatterplot in Figure 5.1 that there is a linear relationship between the group means. Thus, we could have either data from the relative model or data from the absolute model in the case of no interaction effect. In the following we use the relative model.

The regression analyses within the groups give the following results:

Group	m_0	m_1
1	$\hat{y} = 11.2 + 4.52\,(x - \bar{x}_1)$	
2	$\hat{y} = 15.2 + 7.17\,(x - \bar{x}_2)$	
3	$\hat{y} = 21.3 + 7.94\,(x - \bar{x}_3)$	
4	$\hat{y} = 25.0 + 11.94\,(x - \bar{x}_4)$	
5	$\hat{y} = 30.6 + 14.47\,(x - \bar{x}_5)$	

The constants and the intercepts vary a great deal across the five groups, and this is an indication that group memberships should be considered to understand the relationship between Y and X more fully.

In the following we use the model that specifies that the group constants and slopes are linear functions of the group means of X. This is only one of many possible models that can be used to explain why the groups have different intercepts and slopes, and we could have used a variety of group level variables.

When we use the separate equations estimation procedure and regress the observed constants and slopes on the group means of X, we get these estimates of the effect parameters together with their standard errors in parentheses below:

$$m_{0j} = 20.7 + 4.86\,(\bar{x}_j - \bar{x}) + u_j \qquad m_{1j} = 9.21 + 2.47\,(\bar{x}_j - \bar{x}) + v_j \quad [5.4]$$
$$\phantom{m_{0j} = 2}(0.28)\ \ (0.20) \qquad\qquad\qquad \phantom{m_{1j} = 9}(0.37)\ \ (0.26)$$

The coefficient $b_1 = 10.0$ shows that there is an individual-level effect of X present in these data. The coefficient $b_2 = 5.7$ shows that there is a group-level effect of X present, and the coefficient $b_3 = 2.0$ shows that there is an individual-group interaction effect present as well. All three coefficients are significantly different from zero. We also see that each of the four estimates is within two standard errors of the true parameter values.

The single equation regresses Y on the individual, group, and interaction variables. This analysis results in the equation

$$y_{ij} = 20.7 + 9.21\,(x_{ij} - \bar{x}_j) + 4.85\,(\bar{x}_j - \bar{x}) - 2.47\,(x_{ij} - \bar{x}_j)\,(\bar{x}_j - \bar{x}) + f_{ij}.$$
$$\phantom{y_{ij} = }(0.65)\ \ (0.46) \qquad\qquad (0.46) \qquad\qquad (0.32) \qquad\qquad\qquad [5.5]$$

The standard errors are shown in parentheses below the coefficients. The coefficient $B_1 = 9.21$ shows that there is an individual-level effect of X present in these data. The coefficient $B_2 = 4.85$ shows that there is a group-level effect of X present, and the coefficient $B_3 = 2.47$ shows that there is an individual-group interaction effect present. All three coefficients are significantly different from zero. We also see that each of the four estimates is within two standard errors of the true parameter values.

When we compare the estimates from the separate equations in Equation 5.4 with the estimates from the single equation in Equation 5.5, we see that the separate-equations estimates are all equal to the single-equation estimates because the three explanatory variables in Equation 5.5 are uncorrelated with each other. In addition, the standard errors for the estimates from the single equation are all larger than the standard errors from the separate-equation estimates. It is more common for the standard errors from the single equation to be smaller than the standard errors from the separate equations, because the number of data points for the analysis of each separate equation is only equal to the number of groups, whereas the single-equation analysis is based on all individual data points. In this example, there is a fairly large residual sum of squares within each group, but the estimated constants and slopes within the groups are quite close to the true values. This produces the smaller standard errors for the separate-equation estimates than the single-equation estimates.

The estimates and their standard errors are illustrated in Figure 5.3. The figure shows the true values of the three effect parameters, marked by vertical lines. The estimates from the separate equations are shown as bs, and the estimates from the single equation are shown as Bs. For each estimate there is a corresponding 95% confidence interval.

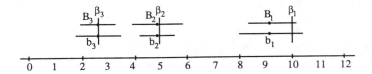

Figure 5.3. True and Estimated Parameter Values, with 95% Confidence Values

We see from the graph that each of the six confidence intervals contains the corresponding true parameter value. The confidence intervals vary in length because of the different magnitudes of the standard errors of the estimates. But, although the standard errors for the estimates from the separate equations are smaller than the standard errors for the estimates from the single equation, only two of the confidence intervals for the separate-equation estimates are smaller than the corresponding confidence intervals for the single-equation estimates. The t values for the confidence intervals for the separate-equations estimates are based on only 3 degrees of freedom, whereas the t values for the single-equation estimates are based on 21 degrees of freedom, and with fewer degrees of freedom the ts are larger. It is much more common to get smaller confidence intervals for all three parameters for the single-equation estimates than for the separate-equations estimates. For example, in Figure 5.2 all three estimates from the single equation have shorter confidence intervals than the estimates from the separate equations.

Next, we want to assess how large the effects on Y of the three explanatory variables are. This is not as problematic here as with the absolute model, because for the relative model the three explanatory variables are usually uncorrelated.

One thing we can do is to compute the standardized regression coefficients for the three variables and compare them. This gives the following estimates:

$$z_y = 0.82 z_{ind} + 0.43 z_{gr} + 0.31 z_{int} + f. \qquad [5.6]$$

According to these three standardized coefficients, the individual-level variable is the most important variable, because it has the largest standardized coefficient. The group and interaction effects are smaller, and the interaction variable has less effect than the group variable.

Another thing we can do is to partition the regression sum of squares into three components. There is a unique way of doing that here, because the three effect variables are uncorrelated. Table 5.4 shows the various regression sums of squares.

By regressing Y on each of the three variables we get the sums of squares in Table 5.4. By regressing Y on all three variables we get a regression sum of squares on 3 degrees of freedom, and that regression sum of squares is the sum of the three sums of squares in the table. The residual sum of squares comes from the multiple regression

TABLE 5.4
Regression Sums of Squares

Variable	Sum of Squares	Proportion
Individual	4,239	0.68
Group	1,175	0.19
Interaction	609	0.10
Residual	221	0.03
Total	6,244	1.00

using all three variables. The table shows that the individual-level variable has the largest effect, followed by the group and then the interaction variables. This is the same pattern we see in the standardized regression coefficients.

With these data generated by the relative model, it also is possible to find the various sums of squares discussed in Table 4.1. When we compute those sums of squares we find the results shown in Table 5.5. From the columns of the table, we see that most of the unexplained variation comes from individual-level variables, and that there is very little unexplained variation from group-level variables. From the rows of the table we see that individual-level variables have a higher unexplained variation both in absolute value and in percentage value, and the interaction variables have the next highest unexplained variation. There is almost no unexplained variation in the group variables.

TABLE 5.5
Explained and Unexplained Sums of Squares for the Three Effects

Source	Explained	Unexplained	Sum
Individual	4,239	195	4,434
Group	1,175	6	1,181
Interaction	609	20	629
Sum	6,023	221	6,244

From sums of squares we turn to sums of absolute values, as displayed in Table 4.1. The expressions in Table 4.1 for the effects contain the actual parameter values. When we substitute the estimated

TABLE 5.6
True and Estimated Effects, Based on Sums of Absolute Values

| Source | Estimated | | True | |
	Effect	Proportion	Effect	Proportion
Individual	276	0.49	300	0.51
Group	146	0.26	150	0.25
Interaction	90	0.16	90	0.15
Residual	53	0.09	52	0.09
Total	563	1.00	592	1.00

regression coefficients, we get the effects shown in Table 5.6. Because we know the true values of the parameters, we also can find the true values of the effects based on sums of absolute values. Table 5.6 contains these true effects, as well as the proportions of effects due to the different variables. We see from the table that the estimated and true proportions of effects are very close to each other, meaning that the estimation procedure works well.

Tables 5.4 and 5.6 present two competing ways of assessing the magnitudes of the effects of the individual, group, and interaction variables. The numbers in Table 5.6 are more of a true reflection of the process these 25 individuals were exposed to and that generated the observed values of Y than the numbers in Table 5.4. The sums of squares in Table 5.4 are a byproduct of the classical way of using sums of squares to measure effects in multiple regression. But here those sums of squares do not represent the actual process as well as the sums of absolute values, and we take the numbers in Table 5.6 to represent better the magnitudes of the effects. From the results in Table 5.6 we find that the individual-level variable accounts for about half of the effect on Y. The effect of the group variable is half that of the individual variable, and the effect of the interaction variable is about one third that of the individual variable. The model fits well, and there is a very small effect of the residual variable.

6. CENTERING

How large the effects are of the individual, group, and interaction variables is often an important question. The data were generated by some process, and we try to create equations that reflect that process. The equations for the absolute and relative models in earlier chapters are two examples of such processes. The measurements of effects that best reflect those processes are the sums of the absolute values of the variables multiplied by the absolute values of the parameter estimates. These sums tell us how far the values of Y were moved as the individuals were exposed to the different variables.

At the same time, regression analysis has a long history of measuring effects of variables by sums of squares, mainly because sums of squares, together with their degrees of freedom, add up in a nice way to total sums of squares and total degrees of freedom. On a more theoretical level, sums of squares have nice expected values that show how the sums of squares can be used for statistical inference. However, this does not prove that sums of squares are the only or the best way of measuring magnitudes of effects. One drawback is that small numbers stay small when they are squared, whereas large numbers get much larger when they are squared. Thus, different observations contribute in very different ways to the sums of squares.

For the relative model, the sums of absolute values and sums of squares involve the same numbers. The only difference is that in one case we add the absolute values and in the other case we add the squares. The results will be different, but conceptually the two measures are not very different.

The problem is much more severe for the absolute model. There, the sums of absolute values and the sums of squares are not even based on the same numbers. The sums of absolute values are based on distances from a no-effect horizontal line. The sums of squares are based on distances from a mean line. In addition, the explanatory variables are correlated, and we do not get unique sums of squares.

This leads us to a search for some other way of measuring effects of the three explanatory variables for the absolute model. It has been suggested that we should subtract the group means and thereby make the variables uncorrelated. But we have shown that such a rescaling of the variables is more than just rescaling the data. Such a subtraction takes us from the absolute to the relative model, and such a change of model cannot be made unless there are good substantive reasons for using a different model.

Another solution has been proposed by Boyd and Iversen (1979). (For a critique of this method see Tate [1984].) The proposal involves centering the data on some common value c. The centering is done in

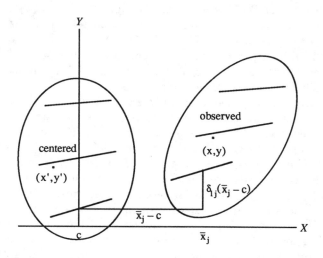

Figure 6.1. Centering Data to a Common Constant c

such a way that the within-group intercepts and slopes are unchanged. From the two model equations (3.8 and 3.9) we know that the information about the three effect parameters is contained in those slopes and intercepts. Thus, anything we do to the data should ensure that the slopes and intercepts do not change.

Figure 6.1 illustrates the way in which the data are centered at the common value of c. Each within-group regression line is moved along its own direction until the mean point is centered on top of $X = c$. Similarly, each observation is moved along the same direction and equally far. This way, an observation with coordinates (x, y) is centered to a new point with coordinates (x', y'). From the way all the data points are moved, we see that regression analyses within each of the groups on the centered data will give the same values of the intercepts and slopes as the old data. Thus, the intercepts and slopes within the groups are preserved by the centering process.

The figure also shows how the coordinates change from the observed to the centered data. From the bottom line we see that the mean point in the jth group moved down and then left onto the vertical axis at $X = c$. The point moved left a distance of $\bar{x}_j - c$, which means that this is the value subtracted from the old value of X.

Similarly, because the slope of the line for this group equals d_{1j}, the point moved downwards a distance of $d_{1j}(\bar{x}_j - c)$. In the centering process all points in this jth group move in the same way. This means that we get the following equations relating the old observations (x, y) and the new, centered observations (x', y'):

$$y'_{ij} = y_{ij} - \delta_{1j}(\bar{x}_j - c) \qquad [6.1]$$

$$x'_{ij} = x_{ij} - (\bar{x}_j - c). \qquad [6.2]$$

The original within group relationship between Y and X is expressed in the equation

$$y_{ij} = \delta_{0j} + \delta_{1j} x_{ij} + \varepsilon_{ij}. \qquad [6.3]$$

By substituting Equation 6.3 into Equation 6.1 we get the following relationship between the new y' and the old x:

$$y'_{ij} = \delta_{0j} + \delta_{1j}(x_{ij} - \bar{x}_j + c) + \varepsilon_{ij}. \qquad [6.4]$$

To compute the centered Y values we need to estimate the within-group intercepts and slopes. One way to do that is simply to regress Y on X within each group. Another way is to use the single equation on the uncentered data and estimate the four alphas, then enter those estimates in the model equations to produce predicted deltas. These estimates of the within-group intercepts and slopes are often better than the separate estimates obtained from each group.

The model equations still specify that the within-group intercepts and slopes are linear functions of the group means of X. But, as in the relative model on uncentered data in Chapter 4, for convenience we subtract the overall mean from the group means. The model equations can then be written

$$\delta_{0j} = \gamma_0 + \gamma_2(\bar{x}_j - \bar{x}) \qquad [6.5]$$

$$\delta_{1j} = \gamma_1 + \gamma_3(\bar{x}_j - \bar{x}). \qquad [6.6]$$

When we substitute the model equations in Equations 6.5 and 6.6 into Equation 6.4, we get the following single equation for the centered data:

TABLE 6.1
Sums of Squares and Proportions of Effects, for Example Centered to 0

Variable	Sum of Squares	Proportion
Individual	2,520	0.40
Group	2,450	0.39
Interaction	1,010	0.16
Residual	237	0.04
Total	6,219	1.00

$$y'_{ij} = \delta_{0j} + \delta_{1j}(x_{ij} - \bar{x}_j + c) + \varepsilon_{ij}$$

$$= [\gamma_0 + \gamma_2(\bar{x}_j - \bar{x})] + [\gamma_1 + \gamma_3(\bar{x}_j - \bar{x})](x_{ij} - \bar{x}_j + c) + \varepsilon_{ij} \qquad [6.7]$$

$$= \gamma_0 + \gamma_1(x_{ij} - \bar{x}_j + c) + \gamma_2(\bar{x}_j - \bar{x}) + \gamma_3(x_{ij} - \bar{x}_j + c)(\bar{x}_j - \bar{x}) + \varepsilon_{ij}$$

The question we now face is what value to use for the constant c. In their original formulation Boyd and Iversen (1979) use $c = 0$. In that case, the single equation reduces to the equation

$$y'_{ij} = \gamma_0 + \gamma_1(x_{ij} - \bar{x}_j) + \gamma_2(\bar{x}_j - \bar{x}) + \gamma_3(x_{ij} - \bar{x}_j)(\bar{x}_j - \bar{x}) + \varepsilon_{ij}. \qquad [6.8]$$

From this equation, we see that when we center the data to the common value of 0, then the centered Y values are analyzed according to the relative model. In that case the three explanatory variables are uncorrelated, and we can get unique sums of squares as measures of the effects of the three variables.

With the example with absolute data from Chapter 5 we get the following results. First, we estimate the five within group slopes according to the equation

$$\hat{d}_{1j} = 21.72 - 2.92\bar{x}_j \qquad [6.9]$$

by using the five group means. With these estimated slopes, we use Equation 6.1 to compute the centered Y values. When we regress the centered Y values on the three explanatory variables in Equation 6.8, we get the sums of squares and proportions shown in Table 6.1.

Compared to the results of the original data reported in the previous chapter, this centering method gives a larger group effect and a

TABLE 6.2

Sums of Squares and Proportions of Effects, for Example with Data
Centered to the Overall Mean of X

Source	Sum of Squares	Proportion	Source	Sum of Squares	Proportion
Individual	2,520	0.37	Individual	2,520	0.37
Group	2,965	0.44	Group after		
Interaction			Interaction	249	0.04
after Group	1,011	0.15	Interaction	3,727	0.55
Residual	240	0.04	Residual	240	0.04
Total	6,736	1.00	Total	6,736	1.00

smaller interaction effect. The basic difference between the centered
and uncentered data is that if the values of X are not near zero, then
this centering process extrapolates and moves the data outside the
range in which they were observed.

One way around this extrapolation is to center the data to some other
value of c. A natural choice is to use $c = \overline{x}$, the overall mean of X. This
eliminates the problem of centering by extrapolation outside the range of
the observed X values. Instead, we bring each group in toward the middle.

In this case the centered values of Y are found according to the
equation

$$y'_{ij} = \delta_{0j} + \delta_{1j} (x_{ij} - \overline{x}_j + \overline{x}) + \varepsilon_{ij} \qquad [6.10]$$

and the single equation for the analysis becomes

$$y'_{ij} = \gamma_0 + \gamma_1 (x_{ij} - \overline{x}_j + \overline{x}) + \gamma_2 (\overline{x}_j - \overline{x}) + \gamma_3 (x_{ij} - \overline{x}_j + \overline{x}) (\overline{x}_j - \overline{x}) + \varepsilon_{ij} . \qquad [6.11]$$

The individual-level variable is uncorrelated with both the group and the
interaction variables. But the group and interaction variables are correlated, and we cannot find a unique sum of square for each of them.

With the absolute data from Chapter 5 we get the following results.
First, we estimate the five within-group slopes according to Equation
6.9. Then, we use these slopes and $c = \overline{x}$ in Equation 6.1 to get the ad-
justed Y values. Those data are used for the regression model expressed in Equation 6.11. The resulting sums of squares and
proportions are shown in Table 6.2.

The results in the left part of Table 6.2 are not very different from the results in Table 6.1 where the data are centered to 0. But when we let the interaction variable enter before the group-level variable, we get very different results. The group effect now is very small, and the interaction effect is larger than the individual-level effect. If we average the effects from the two analyses we get 2,520 (0.37) for the individual-level variable, 1,607 (0.24) for the group-level variable, and 2,369 (0.35) for the interaction variable. These proportions are more in line with the proportions obtained in Chapter 5 from the sums of absolute values for these data.

7. OTHER APPROACHES

Anytime we analyze data organized in groups on one or more levels we perform a multilevel analysis of one kind or another. We can have one set of groups, or we can have data in groups that themselves are nested within other groups. In educational research, for example, we may have data on students within classes. It also is possible to consider a nesting of classes within schools that themselves are within school districts.

With these kinds of data we may be interested simply in whether the groups are different. Such a question can be answered using analysis of variance, and for nested data we can use variance component analysis. When we go beyond the question of whether groups are different to try to understand *why* the groups are different, we move into contextual analysis. Here we take a look at some of the statistical models that lead to contextual analysis, as well as some more complicated contextual models.

Analysis of Variance

The most common approach to the analysis of data from several groups is to perform an analysis of variance. Such an analysis will tell us to what extent the groups are different from each other. If we find a large value of eta squared, we conclude that the categorical variable defining the groups is strongly related to the dependent variable. If we find a large value of the F statistic, we conclude that the group variable has a statistically significant effect.

In analysis of variance we distinguish between fixed (Model I) and random (Model II) models. A fixed model is used when we have data on all the groups we are interested in, and a random model is used when we have data only on a sample of groups. A fixed one-way analysis-of-variance model is expressed in the equation

$$y_{ij} = \mu + \alpha_j + \varepsilon_{ij}. \qquad [7.1]$$

Y is the observed dependent variable, μ is the overall level of Y and is estimated by the overall mean $\overline{y}$. α_j is the effect on Y that comes from belonging to the jth group, and it is estimated by the difference between the group mean and the overall mean ($\overline{y}_j - \overline{y}$). Finally, ε_{ij} is the effect on Y by the residual variable, estimated by the difference between the observed value of Y and the group mean ($y_{ij} - \overline{y}_j$).

A random model is used when we have a large number of groups, and we only collect data on a sample of such groups. Suppose we want to know whether the number of completed years in school is affected by the county in which one lives. Because there are more than 3,000 counties in this country, it is too costly to collect data on a random sample of respondents in each county. However, we can draw a random sample of counties first, and then collect data on respondents within those counties. A random one-way analysis-of-variance model is expressed in the equation

$$y_{ij} = \mu + a_j + \varepsilon_{ij}. \qquad [7.2]$$

The effect of a particular county is now denoted a_j, and in this example there are more than 3,000 a values.

One way to find out whether these as are different, if we had all of them, is to compute their variance. If the variance of the as is larger than zero, then at least some of the as are different from each other, and it makes a difference for education what county one lives in. If we have data on respondents in a sample of counties, then we can only estimate the variance of the as. The variance of the as is estimated from the between- and within-group mean squares. If the estimated variance is larger than zero, we conclude that there is a county effect, and the larger the variance, the larger the effect. Standard least-squares estimation methods for a random model require the number of observations to be the same within each group.

The main drawback of analysis of variance is that group membership is the only explanatory variable. No properties of the individuals or of the groups are taken into account as explanatory variables. Thus, if we find that the groups are different, we still have no sense of the possible reasons for why they are different. Differences between the groups could have occurred because of individual-level variables as well as because of group-level variables. Also, an analysis of variance will not tell us about possible individual-group interaction effects.

Analysis of Covariance

The next step up in complexity is to study the presence of group differences while controlling for an individual-level variable. Suppose, in the example above, we think that the age (X) of the respondent affects the number of completed years of school. With this variable included the model can now be written

$$y_{ij} = \mu + \alpha_j + \beta\, x_{ij} + \varepsilon_{ij}\,. \qquad [7.3]$$

Beta is the regression coefficient for the X variable, and x_{ij} is the age of the ith respondent in the jth group. It also is possible to have more than one individual-level variable in the model. Following the notation in Equation 7.1, we have an alpha term for each group, and there are J fixed alpha values.

One way to perform the analysis is to replace the alphas by $J - 1$ dummy variables, where J is the number of groups, and do a multiple regression analysis with the dummy variables and X. With such dummy variables it also is possible to introduce interaction variables as products of X and the dummy variables. Because of collinearity problems it is often best to do a simple regression analysis of Y on X as well. We then are able to find how much of the overall R square from Equation 7.3 is due to X after we take group membership into account, as well as how much is due to group membership after we take X into account.

It also is possible to think of the county effects as random. We start with Equation 7.2, and we add the control variable X. This gives the model expressed in the equation

$$y_{ij} = \mu + a_j + \beta x_{ij} + \varepsilon_{ij}. \qquad [7.4]$$

The two random parts of Equation 7.4 are the as and the epsilons. We can collect the two random terms and write the equation as

$$y_{ij} = \mu + \beta x_{ij} + (a_j + \varepsilon_{ij}). \qquad [7.5]$$

This two-level model has a random component ε_{ij} from the individual level and a_j from the group level. From this model it is possible to estimate the variances of the as and the epsilons. (For a further discussion of this model see Goldstein [1987].)

The main advantage of analysis of covariance over analysis of variance is that analysis of covariance takes into account the individual-level variable X. The main advantage of analysis of covariance over a regression analysis of Y on X is that it also takes into account group membership. With the analysis of covariance we also can take into account interaction variables. The main drawback is that actual properties of the groups are not taken into account, because we do not include any specific group variables. When we find that the groups are different, we do not know why they are different.

Random Regression Coefficients

Both the absolute and relative contextual models in Chapters 3 and 4 are founded on the basic premise that the regression coefficients within the groups are linear functions of certain group variables. One special case consists of using the group mean of X as the group variable that determines the within-group regression coefficients. The discussion here is presented in terms of the absolute contextual model, but a similar set of equations for the relative model also exists.

In Equation 3.1 we specify that there is a linear relationship between Y and X within each group. For each of the J groups this is expressed in the equation

$$y_{ij} = \delta_{0j} + \delta_{1j} x_{ij} + \varepsilon_{ij}. \qquad [7.6]$$

One possible contextual model specifies that the intercepts and slopes within the groups in Equation 7.6 are linearly related to the group mean of X. This model is specified in Equations 3.8 and 3.9, repeated here:

$$\delta_{0j} = \alpha_0 + \alpha_2 \bar{x}_j \qquad [7.7]$$

$$\delta_{1j} = \alpha_1 + \alpha_3 \bar{x}_j \qquad [7.8]$$

This model consists of two deterministic equations relating the within-group parameters and the contextual variable. However, this does not imply that the estimated deltas we get from regressing Y on X within each group are related deterministically to the contextual variable. The estimated intercept d_{0j} differs from the parameter δ_{0j} by some amount υ_{0j} and the estimated slope d_{1j} differs from the parameter δ_{1j} by some amount υ_{1j}. From this follows that we can estimate the alphas with the two equations

$$d_{0j} = \alpha_0 + \alpha_2 \bar{x}_j + \upsilon_{0j} \qquad [7.9]$$

$$d_{1j} = \alpha_0 + \alpha_2 \bar{x}_j + \upsilon_{1j}. \qquad [7.10]$$

Because of the presence of the residuals in these two equations a scatterplot of the ds and the group means will not show a straight line.

There is not enough evidence in our data to determine whether the deltas and the $\bar{x}$s are related as we have specified in Equations 7.7 and 7.8, because we can only hope to work with the estimated deltas rather than the deltas themselves. This raises the question of whether we should consider other variations of the two model equations. In particular, would the two model equations be a better representation of reality if they contained a random component?

With a random component in the model equations, they can be written

$$\delta_{0j} = \alpha_0 + \alpha_2 \bar{x}_j + \zeta_{0j} \qquad [7.11]$$

$$\delta_{1j} = \alpha_1 + \alpha_3 \bar{x}_j + \zeta_{1j} \qquad [7.12]$$

When these model equations are substituted into Equation 7.6, we get the following single equation for the relationship between the dependent variable and the individual, group, and interaction variables:

$$y_{ij} = \alpha_0 + \alpha_1 x_{ij} + \alpha_2 \bar{x}_j + \alpha_3 x_{ij} \bar{x}_j + (\varepsilon_{ij} + \zeta_{0j} + \zeta_{1j} x_{ij}) \qquad [7.13]$$

This equation contains random components for the individual, group, and interaction effects.

In principle, there are several reasons why we may want to consider models with random regression coefficients within the groups. For one thing, by including residual terms in model Equations 7.11 and 7.12 and thereby making the deltas random, we allow for effects on the within-group regression parameters of a variety of other, unspecified contextual variables in addition to the group mean. Also, by bringing additional residual terms into the model, we should get parameter estimates with smaller standard errors. For a further discussion of models with random regression coefficients, see de Leeuw and Kreft (1986), Goldstein (1987), and Tate and Wongbundhit (1983).

Fixed Versus Random Models

There is not enough evidence in the literature to suggest that it is always necessary to use models with random regression coefficients. If there are strong individual, group, and interaction effects present, there is reason to believe that such effects will be found whether we use a model with random coefficients or one with fixed coefficients. It may be that using random coefficients is a better way to discover small effects, but small effects are not as substantively interesting.

Any result from a statistical analysis is due to two sources. One source is the data themselves, and the other source is the model used to analyze the data. Two different data sets analyzed with the same model will commonly give two different results due to the differences in the data, and the same data set analyzed with two different models will commonly give two different results due to the differences in the models. We want the influences of the model we use to be as small as possible, which argues in favor of using models with fixed parameters when possible. Models with random coefficients are more complicated, and the estimation procedures they require are more involved. Because of this, the effect of the model on the results becomes larger for models with random coefficients than for models with fixed coefficients. The choice between fixed and random coefficients ideally should be made on substantive grounds, but we may not always know enough about the substantive issues to make the choice on that basis.

Computationally, the models with fixed parameters are easier to use than models with random parameters. Ordinary least squares can be used to estimate the parameters and to measure the magnitude of the effects on the different levels. This means that any standard statistical package can be used for the computations. This only becomes cumbersome when we have a large number of groups, and therefore must do many subset analyses. Specialized multilevel computer packages can be more difficult to run, and they are not as readily available for all types of computers.

It also may be that the current state of contextual analysis for many applications is not far enough advanced to require the use of the more sophisticated random models. It may be that our efforts should be directed more toward other areas before we turn to more refined statistical models. One thing we need is a better understanding of the process whereby the membership in a group influences the dependent variable. We also need better definitions of the groups we study. Groups tend to overlap; for example, we belong in a certain neighborhood as well as certain occupational, religious, ethnic, and other groups. We need to sort out which aspects of these groups are relevant for the contextual effects. Also, it may be that we get a better sense of the contextual effects if we have substantive reasons for the inclusion of additional contextual variables. The models here are presented using group means of the individual-level variable as the contextual variable. However, this is only a very special case of contextual analysis, and we may get a better representation of the phenomena we are studying if we are able to include additional variables into the analysis.

Computing

Many of the models discussed above can be analyzed using standard statistical software like SAS and SPSSX. But it can get increasingly difficult to generate the group variables when the models get more complex, the number of groups gets large, and there are more than two levels.

Four major software packages for the analysis of data observed on several levels currently exist. (For a more detailed discussion of these packages, see Kreft and Kim [1990].) The first of these is the GENMOD package from the Population Studies Center of the University of Michigan. It is constructed to do comparative as well as contextual analysis. The HLM package is designed for contextual analysis as well as growth curve analysis, and it may be the package most commonly used in the United States. For a further description, see Bryk, Raudenbush, Seltzer, and Congdon [1988].) The ML3 package comes from the Multilevel Models Project of the Institute of Education, University of London. This package offers the widest choice of input and control over the estimation process. (For a further description see Prosser, Rasbash, and Goldstein [1990].) Finally, the VARCL package does variance component types of analyses. The program was originally written by Aitkin and Longford (1986), and it is maintained by Longford.

REFERENCES

AITKIN, M. A., and LONGFORD, N. (1986) "Statistical modelling issues in school effectiveness studies." *Journal of the Royal Statistical Society* 149A: 1-43.

ALPHEIS, H. (1988) *Kontextanalyse* [Contexual Analysis]. Wiesbaden: Deutscher Univesitäts-Verlag.

APPLE, N., and O'BRIEN, D. J. (1983) "Neighborhood racial composition and residents' evaluation of police performance." *Journal of Police Science and Administration* 2: 76-83.

ASPIN, L. T. (1988) "A contextual analysis of power and foreign policy behavior." *Quality and Quantity* 22: 331-346.

BEDEIAN, A. G., KEMERY, E. R., and MOSSHOLDER, K. W. (1989) "Cross-level research. Testing for cross-level interactions: An empirical demonstration." *Behavioral Science* 34: 70-78.

BLALOCK, H. (1984) "Contextual-effects models: Theoretical and methodological issues," in R. H. Turner and J. F. Short (eds.) *Annual Review of Sociology* 10: 353-372.

BLAU, P. M. (1960) "Structural effects." *American Sociological Review* 26: 178-193.

BLAU, R. R. (1988) "The context of art attendance: The primary sampling unit as the unit of aggregation." *Social Science Quarterly* 69: 930-941.

BOYD, L. H., Jr., and IVERSEN, G. R. (1979) *Contextual Analysis: Concepts and Statistical Techniques.* Belmont, CA: Wadsworth.

BROWN, C. (1982) "The Nazi vote: A national ecological study." *American Political Science Review* 76: 285-301.

BROWN, T. (1981) "On contextual change and partisan attributes." *British Journal of Political Science* 11: 427-447.

BRYK, A., RAUDENBUSH, S. W., SELTZER, M., and CONGDON, R. T. (1988) *An Introduction to HLM: Computer Program and Users Guide.* Chicago: University of Chicago.

DAMUTH, J., and HEISLER, L. (1988) "Alternative formulations of multilevel selection." *Biology and Philosophy* 3: 407-430.

DAVIS, J. A., SPAETH, J. L., and HUSON, C. (1961) "A technique for analyzing the effects of group composition." *American Sociological Review* 26: 215-225.

De LEEUW, J., and KREFT, G. G. (1986) "Random coefficient models for multilevel analysis." *Journal of Educational Statistics* 11: 57-85.

ECKART, D. R., and DURAND, R. (1985) "Contextual variables and policy arguments." *The Social Science Journal* 22: 1-14.

ENGEL, U. (1988) "Status inconsistency and criss-cross in an adolescent society." *International Sociology* 3: 283-300.

ENTWISLE, B., CASTERLINE, J. B., and SAYED, H. A.-A. (1989) "Villages as contexts for contraceptive behavior in rural Egypt." *American Sociological Review* 54: 1019-1034.

ENTWISLE, B., and MASON, W. M. (1985) "Multilevel effects of socioeconomic development and family planning programs on children ever born." *American Journal of Sociology* 91: 616-649.

ESSER, H. (1982) "Sozialräumliche Bedingungen der sprächlichen Assimilation vor Arbeits-migranten" (Socioecological conditions of language-acquisition by migrant workers). *Zeitschrift für Soziologie* 11: 279-306.

ESSER, H. (1986) "Social context and inter-ethnic relationships: The case of migrant workers in West German urban areas." *European Sociological Review* 2: 30-51.

EULAU, H. (1981) "On revolutions that never were," in S. L. Long (ed.) *The Handbook of Political Behavior* (pp.vii-xv). New York: Plenum.

FERNANDEZ, R. M., and KULIK, J. C. (1981) "A multilevel model of life satisfaction: Effects of individual characteristics and neighborhood composition." *American Sociological Review* 46: 840-850.

FINNEY, J. W., and MOOS, R. M. (1984) "Environmental assessment and evaluation research." *Evaluation and Program Planning* 7: 151-167.

FINNEY, J. W., and MOOS, R. M. (1986) "Matching patients with treatments: Conceptual and methodological issues." *Journal of Studies in Alcohol* 47: 122-134.

GATES, L. B., and ROHE, W. M. (1987) "Fear and reactions to crime: A revised model." *Urban Affairs Quarterly* 22: 425-453.

GOLDSMITH, H. F., JACKSON, D. J., KRAMER, M., BRENNER, B., STILES, D. I., TWEED, D. L., HOLZER III, C. E., and MACKENZIE, E. (1986) "Strategies for investigating effects of residential context." *Research on Aging* 8: 609-635.

GOLDSTEIN, H. (1987) *Multilevel Models in Education and Social Research.* New York: Oxford University Press.

GOYDER, J. (1985) "Nonresponse in surveys: A Canada-United States comparison." *Canadian Journal of Sociology* 10: 231-251.

HAUSER, R. M. (1970) "Context and consex: A cautionary tail." *American Journal of Sociology* 75: 645-664.

HAUSER, R. M., and MOSSEL, P. A. (1985) "Fraternal resemblance in educational attainment and occupational status." *American Journal of Sociology* 91: 650-673.

HERO, R. E., and DURAND, R. (1985) "Explaining citizen evaluations of urban services: A comparison of some alternative models." *Urban Affairs Quarterly* 20: 344-354.

HOLZEMER, W. L., JENNINGS, B. M., CHAMBERS, D. B., and PAUL, S. M. (1989) "Contextual regression analysis." *Nursing Research* 38: 124-125.

HOMANS, G. C. (1950) *The Human Group.* Orlando, FL: Harcourt Brace Jovanovich.

HUCKFELDT, R., and SPRAGUE, R. (1987) "Networks in context: The social flow of political information." *American Political Science Review* 81: 1197-1216.

HUGHES, M. (1981) "Theory and research in a dangerous world: Reply to Handel." *Social Forces* 60: 589-592.

IVERSEN, G. R. (1973) "Recovering individual data in the presence of group and individual effects." *American Journal of Sociology* 79: 420-434.

IVERSEN, G. R. (1981) "Group data and individual behavior," in J. M. Clubb, W. H. FLANIGAN, and N. H. ZINGALE (eds.) *Analyzing Electoral History: A Guide to the Study of American Voting Behavior* (pp. 267-302). Beverly Hills, CA: Sage.

KENDALL, P. L., and LAZARSFELD, P. F. (1950) "Problems of survey analysis," in R. K. Merton and P. F. Lazarsfeld (eds.) *Continuities in Social Research: Studies in the Scope and Method of "The American Soldier"* (pp. 133-196). New York: Free Press.

KNOKE, D. (1981) "Commitment and detachment in voluntary associations." *American Sociological Review* 46: 141-158.

KREFT, G. G., and de LEEUW, E. D. (1988) "The see-saw effect: A multilevel problem?" *Quality and Quantity* 22: 127-137.

KREFT, G. G., and KIM, K.-S. (1990) "GENMOD, HLM, ML2 and VARCL, four statistical packages for hierarchical linear regression," in P. van den Eeden, J. Hox, and J. Hauer (eds.) *Theory and Model in Multilevel Research: Convergence or Divergence?* (pp. 165-189). Amsterdam: Stichting Interuniversitair Instituut voor Sociaal-Wetenschappeljjk Onderzoek (SISWO).

LANCASTER, T. D., and LEWIS-BECK, M. S. (1989) "Regional vote support: The Spanish case." *International Studies Quarterly* 33: 29-43.

LEEGE, D. C., and WELCH, M. R. (1989) "Catholics in context: Theoretical and methodological issues in studying American Catholic parishioners." *Review of Religious Research* 31: 132-148.

MARKHAM, S. E. (1988) "Pay-for-performance dilemma revisited: Empirical example of the importance of group effects." *Journal of Applied Psychology* 73: 172-180.

MASON, W. M., WONG, G. Y., and ENTWISLE, B. (1983) "Contextual analysis through the multilevel linear model," in S. Leinhardt (ed.) *Sociological Methodology* (pp. 72-103). San Francisco: Jossey-Bass.

MASTEKAASA, A., and MOUM, T. (1984) "The perceived quality of life in Norway: Regional variations and contextual effects." *Social Indicators Research* 14: 385-419.

MUELLER, S. A., and O'BRIEN, D. J. (1986) "Neighborhood racial composition and the utilization of public service." *Sociological Focus* 19: 61-75.

O'BRIEN, J., and ROACH, M. J. (1984) "Recent developments in urban sociology." *Journal of Urban Sociology* 10: 145-170.

PERRY, D. K. (1988) "Implications of a contextualist approach to media-effects research." *Communication Research* 15: 246-264.

PROSSER, R., RASBASH, J., and GOLDSTEIN, H. (1990) *ML3. Software for Three Level Analysis. Users' Guide.* London: University of London.

PRYSBY, C. L. (1989) "Attitudes of southern Democratic party activists toward Jesse Jackson: The effect of local context." *Journal of Politics* 51: 305-318.

RAUDENBUSH, S., and BRYK, A. S. (1986) "A hierarchical model for studying school effects." *Sociology of Education* 59: 1-17.

SCHISSEL, B., WANNER, R., and FRIEDERES, J. S. (1989) "Social and economic context and attitudes toward immigrants in Canadian cities." *International Migration Review* 23: 289-308.

SCHUESSLER, K. (1969) "Covariance analysis in sociological research," in E. F. Borgatta (ed.) *Sociological Methodology* (pp. 219-244). San Francisco: Jossey-Bass.

SELLE, P. (1984) "Religion, class, and ecological analysis: A review." *Acta Sociologica* 27: 377-383.

SIMCHA-FAGAN, O., and SCHWARTZ, J. E. (1986) "Neighborhood and delinquency: An assessment of contextual effects." *Criminology* 24: 667-703.

SMITH, D. A., and JARJOURA, G. R. (1989) "Household characteristics, neighborhood composition and victimization risk." *Social Forces* 68: 621-640.

STIPAK, B. (1980) "Analysis of policy issues concerning social integration." *Policy Sciences* 12: 41-60.

STIPAK, B., and HENSLER, C. (1982) "Statistical inference in contextual analysis." *American Journal of Political Science* 26: 151-175.

TATE, R. L. (1984) "Limitations of centering for interactive models." *Sociological Methods and Research* 13: 251-271.

TATE, R. L. (1985) "Methodological observations on applied behavioral science." *Journal of Applied Behavioral Science* 21: 221-234.

TATE, R. L., and WONGBUNDHIT, Y. (1983) "Random versus nonrandom coefficent models for multilevel analysis." *Journal of Educational Statistics* 8: 103-120.

TREIBER, B. (1980) "Mehrebenenanalysen in der Bildungsforschung" (Multilevel analyses of individual educational research). *Zeitschrift für Entwicklungspsychologie und Pädagogische Psychologie* 12: 358-386.

TREIBER, B. (1981) "Bildungseffekte in Mehrebenenanalysen individueller Schulleistungen" (Class effects in multilevel analyses of individual school performance). *Zeitschrift für Entwicklungspsychologie und Pädagogische Psychologie* 13: 217-226.

USUI, W., and KEIL, T. J. (1987) "Life satisfaction and age concentration of the local area." *Psychology and Aging* 2: 30-35.

van den EEDEN, P., and HÜTTNER, H. J. M. (1982, Winter) "Multi-level research." *Current Sociology* 30(3): 1-181.

VANDERBOK, W. G. (1990) "Critical elections, contained volatility and the Indian electorate." *Modern Asian Studies* 24: 173-194.

WALD, K. D., OWEN, D. E., and HILL, S. S. (1988) "Churches as political communities." *American Political Science Review* 82: 531-548.

WAXMAN, H. C., and EASH, M. J. (1983) "Utilizing students' perception and context variables to analyze effective teaching: A process-product investigation." *Journal of Educational Research* 76: 321-325.

WEATHERFORD, M. S. (1983) "Evaluating economic policy: A contextual model of the opinion formation process." *Journal of Politics* 45: 866-888.

WIENOLD, G., ACHTENHAGEN, F., VAN BUER, J., OLDENBÜRGER, H. A., RÖSNER, SCHLUROFF, M., and WELGE, P. K. G. (1982) "Lernmaterial und Lehrerverhalten in institutionalisierten Leht-Lern-Prozessen—am Beispiel des Englischanfangsunterrichts" (Teaching material and teacher behavior in institutionalized teaching-learning-process, as examplified by beginning English instruction). *Zeitschrift Pädagogik* 28: 545-562.

WIESE, W. (1986) "Schuliche Umwelt und Chancenverteilung" (School environment in higher secondary education). *Zeitschrift für Soziologie* 15: 188-209.

WILLMS, J. D. (1986) "Social class segregation and its relationship to pupil's examination results in Scotland." *American Sociological Review* 51: 224-241.

WILLMS, J. D., and CUTTANCE, P. (1985) "School effects in Scottish secondary schools." *British Journal of Sociology of Education* 6: 289-306.

ABOUT THE AUTHOR

GUDMUND R. IVERSEN is Professor of Statistics and Director of the Center for Social and Policy Studies at Swarthmore College. He received M.A.s in mathematics and sociology from the University of Michigan, and his Ph.D. in statistics from Harvard University. He is participating in several activities trying to improve the teaching of statistics, and his research interests include contextual analysis, Bayesian statistical inference, and the application of statistics to the social sciences in general.

Quantitative Applications
in the Social Sciences

(a Sage University Papers Series)

$8.50 each

SAGE PUBLICATIONS, INC.
P.O. BOX 5084
NEWBURY PARK, CALIFORNIA 91359—9924